★ All-Star

Workbook

Linda Lee ★ Kristin Sherman ★ Stephen Sloan ★ Grace Tanaka ★ Shirley Velasco

Workbook by Kristin Sherman

McGraw-Hill

All-Star 2 Workbook

Published by McGraw-Hill ESL/ELT, a business unit of The McGraw-Hill Companies, Inc. 1221 Avenue of the Americas, New York, NY 10020. Copyright © 2005 by The McGraw-Hill Companies, Inc. All rights reserved. No part of this publication may be reproduced or distributed in any form or by any means, or stored in a database or retrieval system, without the prior written consent of The McGraw-Hill Companies, Inc., including, but not limited to, in any network or other electronic storage or transmission, or broadcast for distance learning.

8 9 10   QPD   10 09 08 07
ISBN-13: 978-0-07-284675-1
ISBN-10: 0-07-284675-5

2 3 4 5 6 7 8 9 10   QPD   10 09 08 07 06
ISBN-13: 978-0-07-111727-2
ISBN-10: 0-07-111727-X

Editorial director: Tina B. Carver
Executive editor: Erik Gundersen
Developmental editors: Jennifer Monaghan, Mari Vargo
Editorial assistant: David Averbach
Production manager: Juanita Thompson
Interior designer: Wee Design Group
Cover designer: Wee Design Group
Illustrator: Andrew Lange, Jerry Zimmerman
Photo Credits: All photos are courtesy of Getty Images Royalty-Free Collection with the exception of the following: Page 2 © Bettmann/CORBIS; Page 54 © Marc Brasz/CORBIS; Page 130 © Bob Rowan; Progressive Image/CORBIS; Page 138 © Erik Dreyer/Getty Images.

International Edition ISBN: 0-07-111727-X
Copyright © 2007. Exclusive rights by The McGraw-Hill Companies, Inc. for manufacture and export. This book cannot be re-exported from the country to which it is sold by McGraw-Hill. The International Edition is not available in North America.

McGraw-Hill

The *McGraw·Hill* Companies

All-Star is a four-level, standards-based series for English learners featuring a picture-dictionary approach to vocabulary building. "Big picture" scenes in each unit provide springboards to a wealth of activities developing all of the language skills. Each *All Star* Workbook unit provides 14 pages of supplementary exercises for its corresponding Student Book unit. The Workbook activities offer students further practice in developing the language, vocabulary, and life-skill competencies taught in the Student Book. Answers to the Workbook activities are available in the Teacher's Edition.

Features

★ **Wide range of exercises** can be used by students working independently or in groups, in the classroom, with a tutor, or at home. Each lesson includes at least one activity which allows students to interact, usually by asking and answering questions.

★ **Alternate application lessons** complement the Student Book application lesson, inviting students to tackle work, family, and/or community extension activities in each unit. Each application lesson concludes with a *Take It Outside* activity, encouraging students to use the language skills they've learned in the unit to interact with others outside of the classroom. Some application lessons also have suggestions for a web-based activity. These *Take It Online* activities help students build computer skills while expanding on the content and the language skills they learned in the unit.

★ **Student Book page references** at the top of each Workbook page show how the two components support one another.

★ **Practice tests** at the end of each unit provide practice answering multiple-choice questions such as those found on the CASAS tests. Students are invited to chart their progress on these tests on a bar graph on the inside back cover.

★ **Spotlight: Grammar** lessons appear at the end of every other unit, offering supplementary grammar practice.

★ **Crossword puzzles and word searches** reinforce unit vocabulary.

Alternate Application Lessons (work, family, community)

Equipped for the Future (EFF) is a set of standards for adult literacy and lifelong learning, developed by The National Institute for Literacy (www.nifl.gov). The organizing principle of EFF is that adults assume responsibilities in three major areas of life — as workers, as parents, and as citizens. These three areas of focus are called "role maps" in the EFF documentation.

Lesson 6 in each unit of the Student Book provides a real-life application relating to one of the learners' roles. The Workbook includes two lessons, each of which addresses the other roles. This allows you, as the teacher, to customize the unit to meet the needs of your students. You can teach any or all of the application lessons in class. For example, if all your students work, you may choose to focus on the work applications. If your students have diverse interests and needs, you may have them work in small groups on different applications. If your program provides many hours of classroom time each week, you have enough material to cover all three roles.

Contents

What's his last name?

LESSON 1

A Complete the sentences.

birth certificate ✓	building pass	diploma	driver's license

1. A _birth certificate_ is a piece of paper that tells a person's date of birth and birthplace.

2. To drive a car, you need a _____.

3. When you finish high school, you receive a _____.

4. You need a _____ to enter some workplaces.

B Read the story. Match the questions and answers below.

It is 1962:

John Fitzgerald Kennedy is the 35th President of the United States. He was born on May 29, 1917 in Brookline, Massachusetts. He has blue eyes and brown hair. He lives at 1600 Pennsylvania Avenue in Washington, DC. That's the White House. The president always lives in the White House.

Questions

1. What is Kennedy's first name?
2. What is his address?
3. What is his birthplace?
4. What is his date of birth?
5. What is his eye color?
6. What is his hair color?

Answers

a. brown
b. John
c. 5/29/1917
d. 1600 Pennsylvania Avenue
e. Brookline, MA
f. blue

C Complete the sentences. Write *live, lives, have,* or *has.*

1. Linda _____*has*_____ brown hair.

2. Jamal and Farah _____ in Chicago.

3. My mother and I _____ on Houston Street.

4. Our teacher _____ blue eyes.

5. Ming _____ a driver's license.

6. They _____ building passes.

7. You _____ a high school diploma.

8. She _____ in New York now.

9. I _____ two brothers.

10. They _____ in Panama.

D Answer the questions about you.

1. What is your eye color? _____

2. What is your hair color? _____

3. What is your address? _____

4. What is your date of birth? _____

5. What is your middle name? _____

6. What is your height? _____

E Check the information you can find on these documents.

Birth Certificate
- ☐ address
- ☑ birthplace
- ☐ date of birth
- ☐ height
- ☐ weight
- ☐ photo

Driver's License
- ☐ address
- ☐ birthplace
- ☐ date of birth
- ☐ height
- ☐ weight
- ☐ photo

LESSON 2

She has curly brown hair.

A Match the pictures and the descriptions. Write the names on the lines.

Adam

Berta

Cristina

Dan

Eli

1. She has straight gray hair and blue eyes.   *Cristina*
2. He has a gray beard and a mustache. He is bald.   _____
3. He has short blond hair and green eyes.   _____
4. She has long curly brown hair and brown eyes.   _____
5. He has long straight brown hair and brown eyes.   _____

B Compare Dan and Cristina. Write 2 more things in each place.

Dan only

He is a man.

1.

2.

Dan and Cristina

They don't have beards.

1.

2.

Cristina only

She is a woman.

1.

2.

C Complete the sentences. Write *have, has, don't have,* or *doesn't have.*

1. Eli _____ *doesn't have* _____ brown hair.
2. Dan _____ blond hair.
3. Adam and Cristina _____ gray hair.
4. Berta _____ curly hair.
5. Cristina _____ curly hair.
6. Eli and Cristina _____ brown eyes.
7. Adam and Cristina _____ long hair.

D Complete the sentences. Write *is, are, has,* or *have.*

1. Cristina's eyes _____*are*_____ blue.

2. Berta _____ slim.

3. Dan _____ medium weight.

4. Berta _____ brown hair.

5. Berta and Dan _____ long hair.

E Answer the questions about you. Use complete sentences.

1. What color are your eyes? _____

2. Do you have brown hair? _____

3. Do you have long or short hair? _____

4. Is your hair curly or straight? _____

5. Are you tall? _____

F Compare yourself and a classmate. Write 2 things in each place.

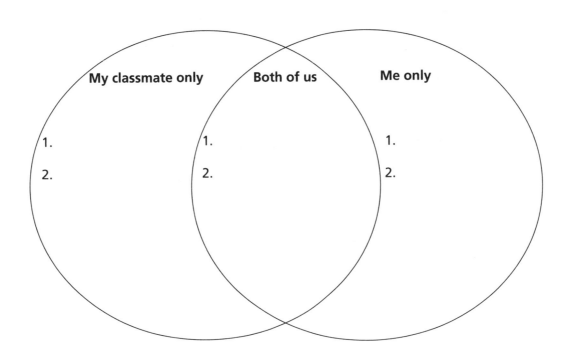

My classmate only

Both of us

Me only

1.

2.

1.

2.

1.

2.

3
LESSON

He looks tired.

A Find these words in the puzzle. Circle them.

afraid   nervous

angry   radio

basketball   relaxed

bored   sad

camera   slide

cell phone   swing

happy   tired

laptop   toy

```
c  e  l  l  p  h  o  n  e  m  a  x  z  e
b  a  s  k  e  t  b  a  l  l  f  g  d  n
o  l  a  s  t  o  a  n  p  g  r  a  y  b
r  f  d  e  j  y  l  g  c  n  a  r  s  w
e  t  i  r  e  d  d  r  a  d  i  o  u  k
d  i  p  h  a  p  p  y  m  a  d  u  t  o
r  e  l  a  x  e  d  n  e  r  v  o  u  s
l  l  a  p  t  o  p  e  r  s  w  i  n  g
p  l  a  s  l  i  d  e  a  i  r  e  d  x
```

B Complete the sentences. Use words from Activity A.

1. I have a test tomorrow. I'm not relaxed. I'm _____ *nervous* _____.

2. Makar has a _____ game tomorrow.

3. My brother likes to take pictures. He has a good _____.

4. Ruth calls me every day. She has a _____.

5. She doesn't sleep well. She is always _____.

6. You don't look happy today. Are you _____?

C Circle the correct answer.

1. Would you give these pencils to Carlos?
   A. I'm sorry. I don't know Carlos. B. That's too bad.

2. Gregory is happy about his new laptop.
   A. I'm sorry. B. That's nice.

3. You can't miss her. She has long hair.
   A. Is it blond or brown? B. What's his name?

4. Ivan is heavy and has short curly hair.
   A. Short curly hair? B. Too bad.

5. Long brown hair?
   A. I'm sorry. B. Right.

6. Laura looks afraid.
   A. She is. She's angry about the test. B. She is. She's nervous about the test.

D Answer the questions about you.

EXAMPLE: When are you happy?   _I'm happy when I'm with my friends._

1. When are you nervous?   _____

2. When are you tired?   _____

3. When are you angry?   _____

4. When are you relaxed?   _____

LESSON

Likes and Dislikes

A Write the words under the pictures.

baseball	housework ✓	loud noises	motorcycle
music	pets	soccer	swimming

1.

_____ *housework* _____

2.

_____

3.

_____

4.

_____

5.

_____

6.

_____

B Match the questions and answers.

Questions	Answers
1. Do you like music?	a. No, she doesn't.
2. Does Molly like baseball?	b. Yes, he does.
3. Do they have pets?	c. Yes, I do.
4. Does Joe like housework?	d. No, we don't.
5. Do we have a book on swimming?	e. No, you don't.
6. Do I need a motorcycle?	f. No, they don't.

C Read the bio poem and check *yes* or *no*.

Sophie

short, nice, good-looking
likes music, food, and people
is happy with family
and friends
is afraid of tests, loud
noises, and dogs

Charbit

1. The woman's name is Sonya. ☐ yes ☑ no
2. She likes dogs. ☐ yes ☐ no
3. She likes her family. ☐ yes ☐ no
4. She doesn't like loud noises. ☐ yes ☐ no
5. Her last name is Charbit. ☐ yes ☐ no
6. She doesn't like food. ☐ yes ☐ no

D Draw a picture of yourself or someone in your family. Complete the bio poem.

_____ (first name)

_____ (3 adjectives)

likes _____ (3 things)

is happy with _____ (2 things)

is afraid of _____ (3 things)

_____ (last name)

WORK

LESSON

He will be late.

A Read the message. Check *yes, no,* or *I don't know.*

TO _Anna_

DATE _2/13/05_   TIME _10:30 a.m._

WHILE YOU WERE OUT

M r. _Sergei Andronovich_

OF _CTI Bank_

PHONE _555-6437_

☑ telephoned   ☐ please call

☐ returned your call   ☐ will call back

MESSAGE _He will be 20 minutes_
late for the meeting.

1. Sergei Andronovich called Patricia.	☐ yes	☑ no	☐ I don't know.
2. He will be late for a meeting.	☐ yes	☐ no	☐ I don't know.
3. Anna called Sergei Andronovich.	☐ yes	☐ no	☐ I don't know.
4. Sergei works with Anna.	☐ yes	☐ no	☐ I don't know.
5. He called in the morning.	☐ yes	☐ no	☐ I don't know.
6. Sergei wants Anna to call him back.	☐ yes	☐ no	☐ I don't know.

B Answer the questions.

1. What date did Sergei call?   _2/13/05_

2. What time did he call?   _____

3. Why did Sergei call?   _____

4. What is his telephone number?   _____

5. Where does Mr. Andronovich work?   _____

C Read the information. Complete the message form.

Henry Temple called Lena Vye on June 6th, 2005. He wants Lena to call him back. His telephone number is 555-7855. Henry works at Southside Adult School. He wants to talk to Lena about her class. He called at 11:00 A.M.

TO _Lena Vye_

DATE _____ TIME _____

WHILE YOU WERE OUT

M _____

OF _____

PHONE _____

☐ telephoned   ☐ please call

☐ returned your call   ☐ will call back

MESSAGE _____

_____

_____

★ ★

TAKE IT OUTSIDE: Practice taking a message with a family member, friend, or coworker. Write the information on the message form.

TO _____

DATE _____ TIME _____

WHILE YOU WERE OUT

M _____

OF _____

PHONE _____

☐ telephoned   ☐ please call

☐ returned your call   ☐ will call back

MESSAGE _____

_____

_____

★ ★

FAMILY

LESSON

What is your child's first language?

A Read the information. Complete the sentences below.

<hr>

WILSON PUBLIC SCHOOLS

Administration Building
2311 Hays St. • Wilson, TX

Language Questionnaire

To Parents: Please answer the following questions. This information will help the school district provide appropriate educational services to your child. Thank you for your help.

Part 1: Do you speak a language other than English in your home?   ☑ Yes
   ☐ No

Part 2: If you answered *yes*, please complete the information and questions below.

Lee, Grace, Elizabeth	*9/12/96*
Student's Name (last, first, middle)	Date of Birth (month/day/year)
345 West Hill Avenue	*Wilson*　　　　　*79381*
Street Address	City　　　　　Zip
(806)555-8112	
Phone Number	
Brookside Elementary	*6th*
School	Grade

Please check the answer to each question. If you check "other," please write the name of the language on the line.

1. What is your child's first language?
　　☐ English
　　☑ Other   *Korean*

2. What language do you speak most often to your child?
　　☐ English
　　☑ Other   *Korean*

3. What language does your child speak with his or her friends?
　　☑ English
　　☐ Other

<hr>

1. The student's first name is _Grace_____.
2. Her address is _____.
3. She is in _____ grade.
4. She speaks _____ as her first language.
5. She goes to _____ School.

B Answer the questions.

1. Thomas Moore is a new student in the Wilson Public School District. He and his family speak English only. Do his parents need to complete Part 2?

   _____

2. Maria Rambla speaks Spanish with her parents. What question asks about this (1, 2, or 3)?

   _____

3. Why does the school need this information?

   _____

★ ★

TAKE IT OUTSIDE: Interview a family member, friend, or coworker. Ask the person about his or her child. Complete the form below.

_____   _____
Student's Name (last, first, middle)   Date of Birth (month/day/year)

_____   _____ _____
Street Address   City   Zip

_____
Phone Number

_____   _____
School   Grade

Please check the answer to each question. If you check "other," please write the name of the language on the line.

1. What is your child's first language?   ☐ English
                                                  ☐ Other   _____

2. What language do you speak most often   ☐ English
    to your child?   ☐ Other   _____

3. What language does your child speak with   ☐ English
    his or her friends?   ☐ Other   _____

★ ★

Practice Test

DIRECTIONS: Look at the message form to answer the next 4 questions. Use the Answer Sheet.

TO _____

DATE _____ TIME _____

WHILE YOU WERE OUT

M _____

OF _____

PHONE _____

☐ telephoned   ☐ please call

☐ returned your call   ☐ will call back

MESSAGE _____

_____

_____

Part 1
Part 2

Part 3

Part 4

Part 5

ANSWER SHEET

1 Ⓐ Ⓑ Ⓒ Ⓓ
2 Ⓐ Ⓑ Ⓒ Ⓓ
3 Ⓐ Ⓑ Ⓒ Ⓓ
4 Ⓐ Ⓑ Ⓒ Ⓓ
5 Ⓐ Ⓑ Ⓒ Ⓓ
6 Ⓐ Ⓑ Ⓒ Ⓓ
7 Ⓐ Ⓑ Ⓒ Ⓓ
8 Ⓐ Ⓑ Ⓒ Ⓓ
9 Ⓐ Ⓑ Ⓒ Ⓓ
10 Ⓐ Ⓑ Ⓒ Ⓓ

1. On what part of the form should you write the telephone number of the person who called?

   A. Part 1
   B. Part 2
   C. Part 3
   D. Part 4

2. What part tells you to call the person back?

   A. Part 2
   B. Part 3
   C. Part 4
   D. Part 5

3. On what part of the form should you write the name of the caller?

   A. Part 1
   B. Part 2
   C. Part 3
   D. Part 4

4. Where do you write the date the person called?

   A. Part 2
   B. Part 3
   C. Part 4
   D. Part 5

DIRECTIONS: Choose the correct answer. Use the Answer Sheet on page 14.

5. What is her occupation?
   A. Sandra
   B. 555-6230
   C. nurse
   D. Chicago

6. What does he look like?
   A. He's tall and has a beard.
   B. He's afraid of slides.
   C. Music and swimming.
   D. He dislikes motorcycles.

7. She's very nervous about the test.
   A. That's great.
   B. I don't know.
   C. That's too bad.
   D. Right.

8. This is my friend, Samantha Geyer.
   A. I don't know her.
   B. Not too bad.
   C. Nice to meet you.
   D. Fine, thanks.

9. How's your class?
   A. That's too bad.
   B. Good. I like it.
   C. I don't know them.
   D. And you?

10. How's it going?
   A. To school.
   B. Not too bad.
   C. I'm in your class.
   D. He is.

HOW DID YOU DO? Count the number of correct answers on your answer sheet. Record this number in the bar graph on the inside back cover.

Spotlight: Grammar

SIMPLE PRESENT STATEMENTS	
Regular Verbs I You We **live** in the U.S. They **don't live** in Mexico.	He She **lives** in Canada. It **doesn't live** in Korea.
Irregular Verb: *Have* I You We **have** brown hair. They **don't have** blond hair.	He She **has** blue eyes. It **doesn't have** green eyes.

OTHER IRREGULAR VERBS: *GO* AND *DO*	
I/you/we/they	**he/she/it**
go/don't go	goes/doesn't go
do/don't do	does/doesn't do

A Look at the picture. Complete the sentences. Write *have, has, don't have,* or *doesn't have.*

1. Omar _____*has*_____ dark brown hair.

2. Sara _____ short hair.

3. Omar and Sara _____ straight hair.

4. Sara _____ blond hair.

5. Omar and Sara _____ curly hair.

6. Omar _____ short hair.

7. Omar _____ a mustache.

B Complete the sentences. Use the verbs in parentheses.

1. Kris _____*lives*_____ in Texas. (live)

2. My teacher _____ a new car. (have)

3. I _____ to school every day. (not/go)

4. Jill _____ to work after lunch. (go)

5. Many people _____ in apartments. (live)

6. We _____ homework. (not/do)

7. He _____ to the store every week. (go)

		YES/NO QUESTIONS WITH THE SIMPLE PRESENT			
Do	I	need a driver's license?			
Do	you	read every day?	**Does**	she	have a building pass?
Do	we	like music?	**Does**	he	like motorcycles?
Do	they	live in the U.S.?	**Does**	it	live in Texas?

C Circle the correct answer.

1. _____ you have a car?

   Ⓐ Do   B. Does

2. Does he _____ to school?

   A. goes   B. go

3. _____ your parents live with you?

   A. Do   B. Does

4. Do they _____ a lot?

   A. works   B. work

5. _____ Mary and her sister like movies?

   A. Do   B. Does

D Write the words in the correct order. Then answer the questions.

1. (your parents / Do / like / swimming / ?)

   Do your parents like swimming?

   _____

2. (your teacher / have / blond hair / Does / ?)

   _____

   _____

3. (have / you / blue eyes / Do / ?)

   _____

   _____

4. (speak / well / your classmates / Do / English / ?)

   _____

   _____

5. (Does / have / your classroom / laptops / ?)

   _____

   _____

LESSON 1

Where can you buy stamps?

A Answer the questions.

get something to drink	get cash	fill a prescription
take classes	check out books	mail packages ✓
see a doctor	buy groceries	

1. What can you do at the post office?   *mail packages* _____

2. What can you do at the library?   _____

3. What can you do at the drugstore?   _____

4. What can you do at a supermarket?   _____

5. What can you do at a bank?   _____

6. What can you do at a restaurant?   _____

B Complete the chart.

THINGS I DO EVERY WEEK	THINGS I NEVER DO

C Answer the questions about you.

1. What is the name of your supermarket?   _____

2. How often do you eat at a restaurant?   _____

3. Where do you study?   _____

4. What medical center is near your home?   _____

5. How often do you mail packages?   _____

D Complete the sentences. Write *am, is,* or *are.*

1. Dana and I _____*are*_____ talking on the phone.

2. Jacob and Marie _____ getting something to eat.

3. She _____ using the computer.

4. You _____ working too hard.

5. I _____ cashing my check.

the present continuous

E Look at the pictures. Write 1 sentence about what the people are doing in each picture.

1. _____

2. _____

3. _____

4. _____

19

2 LESSON

How do I get there?

A Look at the picture. Check *True* or *False* below.

1. Go straight to get to 601 North. ☐ True ☑ False
2. Take a left to get to 31 East. ☐ True ☐ False
3. Take a left to get to 985. ☐ True ☐ False
4. Take a right to get to 31 West. ☐ True ☐ False

B Match the questions and answers.

Questions	Answers
1. __e__ What is she doing?	a. He's going to the shopping center.
2. _____ Where is Antonio going?	b. At 10:30.
3. _____ When does the train leave?	c. Most of the students are.
4. _____ Who is eating in class?	d. Maybe three or four times a year.
5. _____ How often do you stay at a hotel?	e. She's reading a book.
6. _____ Why are they late?	f. They don't have a car.

C Answer the questions about you.

How often do you go to:	every day	a few times a week	a few times a month	a few times a year	never
a shopping center?	☐	☐	☐	☐	☐
a community center?	☐	☐	☐	☐	☐
a medical center?	☐	☐	☐	☐	☐
a library?	☐	☐	☐	☐	☐

D Look at the map. Complete the sentences below.

South Blvd.	Midtown Senior Center ☐	☐ Tri-County Medical Center *Lake St.*	Community Center
	Park Shopping Center ▭	Civic Center Todd Hotel ☐	*Park Rd.*
	Fire Station **6th Ave.**	**5th Ave.**	

1. The community center is on the corner of *Lake Street*

    and _____ .

2. The civic center is next to _____ .

3. The fire station is across from _____ .

4. The Midtown Senior Center is on _____ Avenue.

5. Park Shopping Center is between _____ Road

    and _____ Street.

E Answer the questions about you.

1. Is there a drugstore across from your home? _____

2. How many blocks away is a post office? _____

3. What street is your bank on? _____

F Read the example below. Write directions from your home to a place in your community.

Directions from the community center to Park Shopping Center:

    Go right on Lake Street. Go one block west on Lake Street.
Take a left on 6th Avenue. Take a right on Park Road.
Park Shopping Center is across from the fire station.

Directions from your home to _____:

_____

_____

_____

21

3
LESSON

It's next to the information desk.

A Make words from the letters.

| baggage check | snack bar ✓ | information desk |
| newsstand | pay phone | waiting area |

1. b r c n s k a a _____ snack bar _____

2. a a t n w i i e r g a _____

3. a t w e n s d n s _____

4. k g e g c g c e a a b h _____

5. e p o h y p a n _____

6. d i k i t e r m a o s n n f o _____

B Circle the correct answer.

1. Where can I get something to eat?

   Ⓐ At the snack bar. B. At the newsstand.

2. I need to make a phone call.

   A. There's a pay phone over there. B. The train platform is outside.

3. Where can I find a hotel?

   A. In the waiting area. B. Ask at the information desk.

4. Can I buy a ticket here?

   A. You can read the train schedule. B. No. You need the ticket office.

5. Walter wants something to read.

   A. There's a newsstand over there. B. Go to the pay phone.

C Put the conversation in order. Number the sentences from first (1) to last (6).

_____ At the baggage check.

_____ Thank you.

____1____ Excuse me. Where can I check my luggage?

_____ You're welcome.

_____ Where's the baggage check?

_____ It's next to the newsstand.

D Match the actions and the places.

Actions	Places
1. ask a question	a. baggage check
2. buy a ticket	b. snack bar
3. check luggage	c. information desk
4. get a newspaper	d. newsstand
5. get something to eat	e. ticket office
6. wait for a train	f. waiting area

E Answer the questions about you.

1. Where is a pay phone at your school? _____

2. What magazines do you like? _____

3. Can you read a train schedule? _____

4. Is there an information desk at your school? _____

5. Does your town or city have a train station? _____

LESSON 4

Train Schedules

A Read the train schedule. Check *yes* or *no* below.

1	3	⟨⟨ Train Number ⟩⟩		4	2
READ DOWN				**READ UP**	
11:14 P	5:17 A	Savannah		9:59 P	3:31 A
1:43 A	7:48 A	Jacksonville		7:45 P	1:08 A
	9:32 A	Palatka		5:43 P	
	10:21 A	Deland		4:55 P	
	10:41 A	Sanford		4:35 P	
	11:07 A	Winter Park		4:11 P	
	11:34 A	Orlando		3:53 P	
	12:02 P	Kissimmee		3:10 P	
3:26 A		Waldo			11:25 P
4:09 A		Ocala			10:41 P
4:41 A		Wildwood			9:59 P
5:21 A		Dade City			9:25 P
6:43 A		Tampa			8:25 P
7:23 A		Lakeland			7:22 P
7:51 A	12:53 P	Winter Haven		2:27 P	6:58 P
10:13 A	3:22 P	West Palm Beach		12:15 P	4:46 P
10:34 A	3:43 P	Delray Beach		11:49 A	4:13 P
11:02 A	4:15 P	Fort Lauderdale		11:15 A	3:40 P
11:25 A	4:31 P	Hollywood		11:01 A	3:26 P
12:10 P	5:20 P	Miami		10:35 A	3:00 P

1. The #1 train stops in Orlando.   ☐ yes   ☑ no
2. It takes 8 hours to travel from Savannah to Miami.   ☐ yes   ☐ no
3. The #3 train stops in Kissimmee.   ☐ yes   ☐ no
4. It takes less than 5 hours to go from Miami to Tampa.   ☐ yes   ☐ no
5. The #3 trains leaves Savannah in the morning.   ☐ yes   ☐ no
6. The #2 train leaves Miami in the morning.   ☐ yes   ☐ no

B Circle the correct answer.

1. Ben wants to go from Winter Park to Winter Haven. What train should he take?
   A. #1   B. #2   C. #3

2. Your supervisor needs to travel from Miami to Jacksonville. She wants to arrive in the evening. Which train should she take?
   A. #2   B. #4   C. #1

3. You live in Dade City and want to go to Savannah. Which train should you take?
   A. #2   B. #3   C. #4

C Write the cities in the correct place in the chart.

ONLY TRAINS 1 AND 2 STOP THERE	ALL TRAINS STOP THERE	ONLY TRAINS 3 AND 4 STOP THERE
Waldo	Savannah	Palatka

D Answer the questions.

1. The #3 train leaves Fort Lauderdale at 4:15 and arrives in Hollywood at 4:31. How many minutes is the trip? _____

2. The #1 train leaves Fort Lauderdale at 11:02 and arrives in Hollywood at 11:25. How many minutes is the trip? _____

3. Which train takes less time? _____

4. How long does it take the #4 train to go from Sanford to Jacksonville?
   _____

5. How many minutes is it from Ocala to Wildwood?
   _____

25

What is your area code?

A Read the story. Circle all the places.

The Sanchez Family

Frank and Patty Sanchez live in (Galveston,) (Texas) with their son, Victor. Frank comes from Mexico, but Patty is from Houston, Texas. All of Patty's family lives in Texas. Patty's parents still live in Houston. Patty's brother Mike lives in San Antonio. Her brother John lives in Waco. Patty's sister Lisa lives in Dallas. Patty loves her family very much. She visits them often and she calls them every week.

B Complete the sentences.

1. Lisa lives in _____ *Dallas* _____.

2. Patty's _____ live in Houston.

3. Victor lives in _____.

4. _____ is from Mexico.

5. Mike lives in _____.

C Look at the area code map. Write the area codes next to the places below.

1. Austin _____ _512_

2. Dallas _____

3. El Paso _____

4. Waco _____

5. Houston _____

6. Fort Worth _____

D Answer the questions about you.

1. What is your area code? _____

2. Who do you call every week? _____

3. How often do you call your family? _____

★ ★

TAKE IT OUTSIDE: Interview 2 family members, friends, or coworkers. Complete the chart.

WHAT IS THE NAME OF A PERSON YOU CALL OFTEN?	WHAT CITY DOES THE PERSON LIVE IN?	HOW OFTEN DO YOU TALK TO HIM/HER?	WHAT IS THE AREA CODE?

★ ★

WORK

LESSON

It's on the 5th floor.

A Read the story. Circle the words that are new to you.

bicycle	messenger	building directory

Jean Claude, Bicycle Messenger

Jean Claude is a bicycle messenger. He rides all around the city on his bicycle. He delivers important papers to different offices. When Jean Claude goes into a building, he reads the building directory. He checks that he has the correct address in the building.

B Complete the sentences.

1. Jean Claude rides a _____ *bicycle* _____.

2. He is a _____.

3. He checks the _____ to make sure he has the correct address.

C Read the building directory. Answer the questions below.

THE CARSTON BUILDING
723 4TH AVENUE

ABEL COMMUNICATIONS	7TH FLOOR, SUITE 701
BARSTOW INC.	2ND FLOOR, SUITE 220
EDWARDS AND HAYNES	6TH FLOOR, SUITE 600
MILLER ENTERPRISES	3RD FLOOR, SUITE 350
PETRO CHEM	8TH FLOOR, SUITE 800
REVAMP	4TH FLOOR, SUITE 401
TRIDENT CO.	5TH FLOOR, SUITE 550

1. A. What floor is the Trident Company on?

   B. _the 5th floor_____

2. A. What suite is Abel Communications in?

   B. _____

3. A. Is ReVamp on the 6th floor?

   B. _____

4. A. Is Miller Enterprises on the 3rd floor?

   B. _____

5. A. What company is in Suite 220?

   B. _____

★ ★

TAKE IT OUTSIDE: Interview a family member, friend, or coworker. Write the answers.

1. Where do you work?   _____

2. How many floors are in your building?   _____

3. What floor do you work on?   _____

★ ★

REVIEW

LESSON

Practice Test

DIRECTIONS: Look at the telephone directory to answer the next 5 questions. Use the Answer Sheet.

G-18

ANSWER SHEET

1 Ⓐ Ⓑ Ⓒ Ⓓ
2 Ⓐ Ⓑ Ⓒ Ⓓ
3 Ⓐ Ⓑ Ⓒ Ⓓ
4 Ⓐ Ⓑ Ⓒ Ⓓ
5 Ⓐ Ⓑ Ⓒ Ⓓ
6 Ⓐ Ⓑ Ⓒ Ⓓ
7 Ⓐ Ⓑ Ⓒ Ⓓ
8 Ⓐ Ⓑ Ⓒ Ⓓ
9 Ⓐ Ⓑ Ⓒ Ⓓ
10 Ⓐ Ⓑ Ⓒ Ⓓ

GOVERNMENT

CITY/COUNTY
Animal Control......................................704-555-3786
Bus Information.....................................704-555-7433
Garbage, Recycling..............................704-555-7600
Police—Non-Emergencies.....................704-555-3620
Street Maintenance 704-555-0777
Water—Emergency Services..................704-555-9044

STATE
Driver's Licenses..................................704-555-7882
Highway Patrol.....................................704-555-1442

FEDERAL
IRS Federal Tax Information..............1-800-555-8566
Social Security Administration.........1-800-555-9999

1. What number should you call if you want to know what bus goes to your school?

   A. 704-555-3786   C. 704-555-7600

   B. 704-555-7433   D. 1-800-555-1442

2. There is water in your front yard, but you can't get water in the house. What number should you call?

   A. 704-555-3786   C. 1-800-555-9999

   B. 704-555-7433   D. 704-555-9044

3. You need to get a new driver's license. What number should you call?

   A. 704-555-7882   C. 1-800-555-9999

   B. 704-555-7433   D. 704-555-9044

4. There is a dog in your yard. You think the dog is going to bite you. What number should you call?

   A. 704-555-3786   C. 704-555-7600

   B. 704-555-7433   D. 1-800-555-1442

5. What office do you call with telephone number 704-555-7600?

   A. Animal Control   C. Garbage, Recycling

   B. IRS   D. Highway Patrol

DIRECTIONS: Look at the train schedule to answer the next 5 questions. Use the Answer Sheet on page 30.

13 ≪ Train Number ≫ 14				
READ DOWN				**READ UP**
8:25 A		Salt Lake city		5:25 P
9:10 A		Ogden		4:40 P
12:55 P		Twin Falls		12:35 P
2:40 P		Mountain Home		10:55 A
4:00 P		Boise		9:25 A

6. What time does the train leave Salt Lake City?

   A. 5:25 P.M.

   B. 4:40 A.M.

   C. 8:25 A.M.

   D. 4:00 P.M.

7. Where is the #13 train at 2:40 P.M.?

   A. Salt Lake City

   B. Ogden

   C. Twin Falls

   D. Mountain Home

8. What city is the stop before Ogden on the #14 train?

   A. Salt Lake City

   B. Ogden

   C. Twin Falls

   D. Mountain Home

9. How many cities do the trains go to?

   A. 2

   B. 4

   C. 5

   D. 3

10. What time does the #14 train leave Boise?

   A. 5:25 P.M.

   B. 9:25 A.M.

   C. 8:25 A.M.

   D. 4:00 P.M.

HOW DID YOU DO? Count the number of correct answers on your answer sheet. Record this number in the bar graph on the inside back cover.

LESSON

How much do you spend on groceries?

A Complete the sentences.

ACROSS

1. I buy food at the supermarket. I spend $80 on my _____*groceries*_____ every week.
3. The money you pay to take the bus is called _____.
4. Shampoo and toothpaste are called _____.
6. I drive to school. I have a _____.
7. My rent includes _____. I don't have to pay for my gas and electricity.
8. We don't like to use checks or credit cards. We usually pay by _____.
9. The money you pay each month for an apartment is your _____.

DOWN

1. I have a car. I fill it up with _____.
2. My heat is gas, but my stove needs _____.
5. My family likes to go to movies and rent videos. We spend $50 a week on _____.

B Write the words in the crossword puzzle.

```
    ¹G R O C ²E R I E S
             
  3□ □ □ □ □ □
             
        ⁴□ □ □ □ □   ⁵□ □ □ □
             
        ⁶□ □ □
             
 ⁷□ □ □ □ □ □ □ □    ⁸□ □ □ □
             
                    
        ⁹□ □ □ □
```

C Complete the chart.

THINGS I PAY FOR WITH CASH	THINGS I PAY FOR WITH A PERSONAL CHECK	THINGS I PAY FOR WITH A CREDIT CARD	THINGS I PAY FOR WITH A MONEY ORDER

D Match the simple present and simple past verbs.

Simple Present

1. __f__ buy
2. _____ cash
3. _____ fill
4. _____ get
5. _____ give
6. _____ go
7. _____ live
8. _____ mail
9. _____ need
10. _____ study

Simple Past

a. gave
b. went
c. studied
d. cashed
e. mailed
f. bought
g. filled
h. got
i. needed
j. lived

E Circle the correct answer.

simple past statements

1. What did you do yesterday?
   A. I bought groceries.   B. I fill my prescription.

2. Did you study for the test?
   A. No, I went to bed early.   B. No, I study every day.

3. How did you get to school?
   A. I got to school by bus.   B. I get to school by car.

4. What did you do for recreation last week?
   A. We go to the movies.   B. We went to the movies.

33

LESSON 2

Can you change a twenty?

A Write the words under the pictures.

_____   _____ and

                                 _____

B Read the story. Answer the questions below.

Carl went to the drugstore yesterday. He filled a prescription for $15.00. He bought a magazine for $3.50. He needed a toothbrush, so he got that too. It was $2.25. Carl bought razors for $3.89 and shaving cream for $4.29. He gave the salesclerk $50.

1. How much was the prescription? $15.00
2. How much was the magazine? $3.50
3. What did the toothbrush cost? $2.25
4. How much were the razors? $3.89
5. How much did Carl spend on the shaving cream? $4.29
6. What was the total amount?   _____
7 How much did Carl give the salesclerk? _____
8. How much change should Carl get back? _____

C Write *Yes, he did* or *No, he didn't.*

1. Did Carl buy shaving cream?   Yes, he did.
2. Did he buy toothpaste?   _____
3. Did he spend more than $20?   _____
4. Did Carl get more than $30 in change? _____
5. Did he fill a prescription?   _____

34

D Answer the questions about you.

1. Did you go to school yesterday? _____

2. Did you work last year? _____

3. Did your teacher give homework last night? _____

4. Did your family live in California last year? _____

5. Did you use a razor today? _____

E Put the conversation in order. Number the sentences from first (1) to last (5).

_____ Shouldn't that be $6.05?

_____ Can you change a twenty?

___1___ That'll be $13.95 with tax.

_____ You're right. Thanks.

_____ Sure. Your change is $7.05.

F Read the receipt. Complete the sentences.

1. The shampoo costs _____ $3.89 _____.

2. The name of the drugstore is _____.

3. The time of purchase is _____.

4. The _____ costs $5.99.

5. The _____ is 95 cents.

6. The customer paid with _____.

7. The store clerk gave _____ in change.

Parker Drugs

3295 Centrum Parkway

- -
JAN 28 '04   7:43 PM
- -

1 TOOTHBRUSH	2.49
1 SMOOTH SHAVE RAZOR	5.99
1 GARDEN FRESH SHAMPOO	3.89
Subtotal	12.37
Tax	.95
Amt Paid	13.32
Cash	20.00
Change Due	6.68

3 LESSON

I'd like to make a deposit.

A Match the pictures and the sentences. Write the letters on the lines.

A

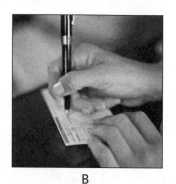

B

C

D

1. She is showing a photo ID. _____C_____

2. He is endorsing a check. _____

3. She is filling out a deposit slip. _____

4. He is giving money to the bank teller. _____

B Complete the sentences.

ATM ✓	bank teller	deposit slip	paycheck
savings account	safe-deposit box	withdrawal slip	checkbook

1. The bank is closed today. You can get money at an _____ *ATM* _____.

2. If you want to take money out of your account, you should fill out a

   _____.

3. I'd like to open a _____, please.

4. Nestor got paid at work today. He needs to deposit his _____.

5. Take this deposit slip to the _____ and she will make sure it
   gets into your account.

C Match the questions and answers.

Questions

1. __c__ Do you have a savings account?
2. _____ Where are the withdrawal slips?
3. _____ What do I need to open a checking account?
4. _____ How can I use the ATM?
5. _____ Do you need a deposit slip?

Answers

a. No, I have one right here.
b. They're on the counter.
c. Not yet. I'd like to open one.
d. You need a photo ID.
e. Use your ATM card.

D Answer the questions about you. Write *Yes, I do, No, I don't, Yes, I did* or *No, I didn't.*

1. Do you have a checking account? _____
2. Did you use an ATM card yesterday? _____
3. Did you get a bank statement for last month? _____
4. Do you have a safe-deposit box? _____
5. Did you get a paycheck for this month? _____

E Write about your experiences with money. Follow the example below.

I have a <u>checking account</u>, but I don't have a savings account. I pay my rent with <u>a check</u>. I also pay for my groceries with <u>a check</u>. I use <u>cash</u> for <u>toiletries and coffee</u>. Last week I bought <u>a radio</u>. I paid with <u>a credit card</u>. Yesterday I bought a <u>magazine</u>. I paid with <u>cash</u>.

LESSON

Checking Accounts

A Read the information. Check *yes* or *no* to the questions below.

Bank of Westville

Contact Us • Help

BANK OF WESTVILLE

SEARCH

| ABOUT THE BANK | ACCOUNTS | BUSINESSES | LOCATIONS |

Be Smart About Your Checking Account

1. If you don't have money in your checking account, don't write checks.
2. Balance your checkbook often. Include ATM withdrawals on your check register.
3. Check your monthly bank statement every month.
4. If two people share one account, have one person keep track of the balance. Keep receipts in a safe place.
5. Use cash for small purchases. The fewer checks you write, the easier it is to keep track.
6. Have your paycheck deposited directly to your account. This way you avoid losing your check.
7. Learn about your account. You should know what fees the bank charges for checks and deduct those fees on your check register.

---

1. It's okay to write checks when there is no money in your account.
   ❑ yes   ☑ no

2. You should check your monthly bank statement.
   ❑ yes   ❑ no

3. You should use cash when you are buying things that don't cost much money.
   ❑ yes   ❑ no

4. You should balance your checkbook often.
   ❑ yes   ❑ no

5. You don't need to write down ATM withdrawals in your check register.
   ❑ yes   ❑ no

B Answer the questions.

wh- questions

1. What should you know about your account?

   You should know what fees the bank charges.

2. When should you check your monthly bank statement?

   _____

3. Where should you write your ATM withdrawals?

   _____

4. Why should you use cash for small purchases?

   _____

C Circle the correct answer.

wh- questions + past tense

1. What did you buy?
   A. a toothbrush   B. last night

2. Where did you write the amount?
   A. to balance my checkbook   B. in my check register

3. Who did you write the check to?
   A. Sim's Drugs   B. I did.

4. Why did you use a check?
   A. in the store   B. I didn't have cash.

5. How much did you pay for it?
   A. every month   B. $1.89

D Answer the questions about you. Write complete sentences.

1. What did you buy last week?

   _____

2. How did you pay for your purchases?

   _____

3. When did you balance your checkbook last?

   _____

COMMUNITY

LESSON

Credit unions are like banks.

A Read the information. Write definitions below.

Credit Unions

Credit unions are like banks in some ways: they offer checking accounts and savings accounts and provide loans. Credit unions are different from banks because members, the people using the credit union, own and run the organization. A credit union is a safe place to save or borrow money.

Many credit unions serve people who do not have a lot of money. They also serve new immigrants. One service that credit unions offer is IRnet. IRnet is a way for people living in the United States to send money back to family in their home countries. It is cheap and safe to transfer money through IRnet.

---

1. credit union: _____

   _____

2. IRnet: _____

   _____

B Check the services that credit unions offer.

- ☑ checking accounts
- ❑ savings accounts
- ❑ monthly statements
- ❑ money transfers
- ❑ loans
- ❑ direct deposit
- ❑ IRnet

C Complete the conversations.

1. A: What services do credit unions offer?

   B: *They offer checking accounts, savings accounts, and loans.*

2. A: How can I send money to my family in another country?

   B: _____

3. A: How are credit unions like banks?

   B: _____

4. A: How are credit unions different from banks?

   B: _____

5. A: Are credit unions safe?

   B: _____

D Answer the question.

Are you interested in a credit union? Why or why not?

_____

_____

_____

★ ★

TAKE IT OUTSIDE OR ONLINE: Find out about credit unions in your area. Look in a telephone directory or use the Internet. Enter "credit unions" + the name of your city or town. Write the name, phone number, and address of 2 credit unions near you.

_____

_____

_____

_____

_____

★ ★

FAMILY

LESSON

They need a good credit history.

A Read the story. Find and circle these words in the story.

| borrow | credit history | down payment |

The Carter Family

Luc and Denise Carter have two children, Sammy and Celeste. Luc is a computer programmer and Denise works part time in a library. Now they are renting an apartment, but they want to buy a house. Luc and Denise need to save money for the down payment on the house. If they can pay 5% of the price of the house, they can borrow the rest of the money from the bank. They need to have a good credit history to borrow money, so they always pay their bills on time. Luc and Denise use a credit card for some things, but they always pay the bill at the end of the month.

B Complete the sentences.

1. Luc and Denise want to buy a _house_____.

2. They need to save money for the _____.

3. They can _____ money from the bank.

4. Sometimes Luc and Denise use a _____, but they always pay it off at the end of the month.

5. You need a good _____ to borrow money.

C Read the sentences. Complete the chart for the Carter family budget.

The Carters pay $850 in rent for their apartment each month.

They spend $400 a month on groceries.

The utilities are $80 a month.

Luc spends $90 a month on a train pass. Denise spends $25 a month on gas.

Sammy and Celeste go to day care two days a week. It costs $300 a month.

Luc and Denise want to save $6,000 in one year, or $500 every month.

The Carter Family Budget

EXPENSE	JANUARY
	$850
food	
train pass	
	$25
	$300
utilities	
savings	
monthly total	

Your Family Budget

EXPENSE	THIS MONTH
monthly total	

D Write your expenses for 1 month in the chart above.

★ ★

TAKE IT OUTSIDE: Interview 2 people who own a home. Complete the chart.

NAME	WHEN DID YOU BUY YOUR HOME?	WHAT PERCENT OF THE COST WAS THE DOWN PAYMENT?	DID YOU BORROW MONEY TO BUY YOUR HOME? IF YES, FROM WHERE?

★ ★

TAKE IT ONLINE: Use the Internet to find information on buying a home for the first time. The U.S Department of Housing and Urban Development has information on buying a home.

Practice Test

DIRECTIONS: Look at the check register to answer the next 5 questions. Use the Answer Sheet.

CHECK REGISTER FOR JACOB GILES

CHECK NO.	DATE	DESCRIPTION OF TRANSACTION	TRANSACTION AMOUNT		DEPOSIT AMOUNT	BALANCE
ATM	4/15	deposit			$700.00	$1039.50
093	4/18	Big Mart	$37.00			$1002.50
094	4/20	South Electric	$68.00			$934.50
095	4/25	rent	$400.00			$534.50
ATM	4/26	Cash withdrawal	$60.00			$474.50

1. What is the date of check # 094?

   A. 4/15

   B. 4/18

   C. 4/20

   D. 4/25

2. What date did he write a check for the rent?

   A. 4/15

   B. 4/18

   C. 4/20

   D. 4/25

3. How much was the electric bill?

   A. $37.00

   B. $68.00

   C. $400.00

   D. $60.00

4. How much money did he take out at the ATM?

   A. $37.00

   B. $68.00

   C. $400.00

   D. $60.00

5. Jacob wants to buy a train ticket for $500. How much money does he need?

   A. $60.00

   B. $34.50

   C. $25.50

   D. $5.50

ANSWER SHEET
1 Ⓐ Ⓑ Ⓒ Ⓓ
2 Ⓐ Ⓑ Ⓒ Ⓓ
3 Ⓐ Ⓑ Ⓒ Ⓓ
4 Ⓐ Ⓑ Ⓒ Ⓓ
5 Ⓐ Ⓑ Ⓒ Ⓓ
6 Ⓐ Ⓑ Ⓒ Ⓓ
7 Ⓐ Ⓑ Ⓒ Ⓓ
8 Ⓐ Ⓑ Ⓒ Ⓓ
9 Ⓐ Ⓑ Ⓒ Ⓓ
10 Ⓐ Ⓑ Ⓒ Ⓓ

DIRECTIONS: Look at the receipt to answer the next 5 questions. Use the Answer Sheet on page 44.

6. What was the date of the purchase?
   A. 12:15
   B. July 19
   C. January 19
   D. July, 1906

```
            Big Mart
        11510 South Blvd.
---------------------------------
JUL 19 '06              12:15 PM
---------------------------------

1 SPARKLE TOOTHPASTE        2.50
1 SMOOTH SHAVE CREAM        3.99
1 SHINY HAIR SHAMPOO        4.99

        Subtotal           11.48
        Tax                  .57
        Amt Paid           12.05
        Cash               12.05
        Change Due           .00
```

7. How did the customer pay?
   A. check
   B. cash
   C. credit card
   D. money order

8. How much was the shampoo?
   A. $2.50
   B. $3.99
   C. $4.99
   D. $11.48

9. How much were the three things together (before tax)?
   A. $2.50
   B. $3.99
   C. $4.99
   D. $11.48

10. How much was the change?
    A. $11.48
    B. $.57
    C. $12.05
    D. zero

HOW DID YOU DO? Count the number of correct answers on your answer sheet. Record this number in the bar graph on the inside back cover.

Spotlight: Grammar

SIMPLE PAST STATEMENTS	
Regular Verbs	**Irregular Verbs**
I You He She It We They } **cashed** my paycheck. **didn't cash** a personal check.	I You He She It We They } **went** to the park. **didn't go** to the bank.

MORE IRREGULAR VERBS			
buy	bought	leave	left
come	came	make	made
eat	ate	pay	paid
do	did	put	put
get	got	read	read
give	gave	see	saw
go	went	spend	spent
have	had	write	wrote

A Write the past tense form of the verbs.

1. do _____*did*_____   5. write _____   9. leave _____

2. put _____   6. read _____   10. visit _____

3. want _____   7. have _____

4. go _____   8. live _____

B Complete the sentences below. Use the verbs in parentheses.

1. I usually _____*go*_____ to work at 9:00 A.M., but yesterday I _____*went*_____ at 7:30 A.M. (go)

2. Our teacher usually _____ a story first, but today she _____ it last. (read)

3. My parents usually _____ me in the summer, but last year they _____ in the spring. (visit)

4. He usually _____ with cash, but last week he _____ for his books with a check. (pay)

5. We usually _____ dinner after 8:00 P.M., but last night we _____ at 7:00 P.M. (eat)

C Rewrite the sentences. Use the past tense.

1. Ben goes to school at 9:00.
   Ben went to school at 9:00

2. He works from 1:00 to 6:00 at the supermarket.

   _____

3. Ben is a cashier.

   _____

4. Most of the customers pay in cash.

   _____

5. Ben makes change.

   _____

46

QUESTIONS WITH THE SIMPLE PAST					
Yes/No Questions			**Wh- Questions**		
Did	I you he she we they	**go** to the bank yesterday?	Who What Where When Why How much How far	**did** **did** **did** **did** **did** **did** **did**	I see yesterday? you do? he cash his check? she leave work? it fall? we spend? they go?

D Match the questions and answers.

Questions

1. Did you work yesterday?
2. Where did they buy their car?
3. What did she do last night?
4. Who did you eat dinner with last night?
5. Did he write you a letter?

Answers

a. No, he didn't. He called.
b. No, I didn't. I was sick.
c. They bought it in New Jersey.
d. I ate with my friend.
e. She went to the movies.

E Answer the questions. Write complete sentences.

1. Who did you call last week?

_____

2. Where did you live five years ago?

_____

3. How many books did you buy last year?

_____

4. How much did you pay for groceries last month?

_____

5. What did you do on Friday night?

_____

LESSON 1

What are your goals?

A Complete the sentences.

be a good parent	get a job
become a U.S. citizen	get a raise
buy a house	get married

1. I would like to work to make money. First, I need to _____.

2. He has a job, but he doesn't make a lot of money. He wants to _____.

3. They don't want to rent an apartment anymore. They want to _____.

4. She moved to the United States 10 years ago. She wants to stay here and

   _____.

5. I had a baby last year. It's important to _____.

B List 5 goals in order of importance to you (*1* is most important).

1. _____

2. _____

3. _____

4. _____

5. _____

C Write the words in the correct order.

EXAMPLE: a university / Makar / graduate / wants to / from / If / she /
get good grades / should

simple present and present conditional

If Makar wants to graduate from a university, she should get good grades.

1. people / buy houses / Many / every year

   _____

2. something new / in school / I / learn / always

   _____

3. If / become a U.S. citizen / you / want to / learn more English / you / should

_____

4. Mani / wants to / study / get good grades / should / if / he

_____

5. get a raise / wants to / If / Sun / work hard / should / she

_____

D Read the graph. Answer the questions below.

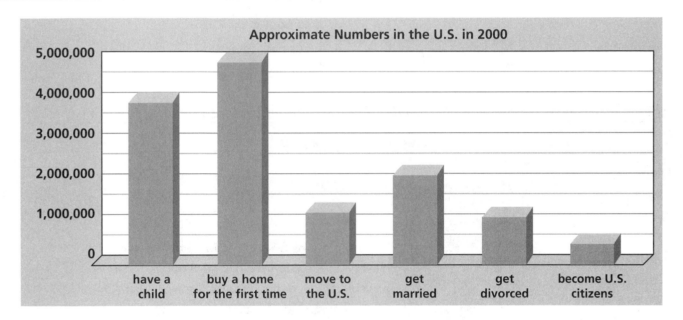

Approximate Numbers in the U.S. in 2000

1. How many people bought a home for the first time in 2000?

   A. about 500,000   c. about 4 million

   B. about 5 million   D. about 2,200,000

2. What did 1.3 million people do in 2000?

   A. had a child   c. became U.S. citizens

   B. got married   D. moved to the United States

3. Which sentence is true?

   A. More people became citizens than got married.

   B. More people bought a home than got married.

   c. More than 5 million people in the U.S. got married.

   D. More people got divorced than got married.

2 LESSON

You should take a business course.

A Match the actions and the things.

Actions	Things
1. go back	a. your children
2. do	b. to school
3. read to	c. money
4. take	d. a computer
5. learn to use	e. a business course
6. save	f. volunteer work

B Look at the website. Check *Yes, No,* or *I don't know* to the questions below.

Welcome to Lake City!

- Immigration
- Housing
- Health
- Community safety
- Child care
- Employment
- Starting a business
- Education, language and literacy
- Human rights
- Social services
- Arts and culture
- Libraries
- City government
- Volunteer opportunities

Welcome to Lake City!

`city search`

We are proud to be one of the fastest growing cities in the region—a city where 100 languages are spoken every day. We are a major business center for the country, and much of our success is due to the many immigrants who chose our city as their new home —a place to live, work, and raise families. We have a lot to offer new residents of our community, including great schools and parks, safe neighborhoods, and exciting business opportunities.

	Yes	No	I don't know.
1. Many people from other countries live in Lake City.	☐	☐	☐
2. Lake City is a major business center.	☐	☐	☐
3. People in Lake City speak more than 300 languages.	☐	☐	☐
4. Lake City has many movie theaters.	☐	☐	☐
5. Lake City doesn't have parks.	☐	☐	☐

C Look at the links on the left side of the website on page 50. Answer the questions.

Which link will give me information if I want to:

1. learn more English? _____

2. do volunteer work? _____

3. buy a house? _____

4. get books to read to children? _____

5. get a job? _____

6. start a business? _____

7. take a business course? _____

D Complete the sentences with *be going to*. Use the verbs in parentheses.

1. I _____ (move) to a different city next year.

2. She _____ (go) back to school in September.

3. We _____ (start) a construction business next summer.

4. They _____ (learn) more English before they become citizens.

5. He _____ (get) a raise next month.

> **future with be going to**

E Write 3 things that you are going to do next week.

EXAMPLE: *I am going to buy a book next week.*

_____

_____

_____

3
LESSON

Who is going to get the job?

A Read the words. Are they the *same*, or the *opposite* in meaning? Circle the correct answer.

EXAMPLE:

tall	short	same	(opposite)
1. last	first	same	opposite
2. bald	no hair	same	opposite
3. long	short	same	opposite
4. hardworking	lazy	same	opposite
5. late	not on time	same	opposite
6. relaxed	nervous	same	opposite
7. good with people	likes people	same	opposite
8. loud	quiet	same	opposite
9. organized	disorganized	same	opposite
10. has a bad attitude	doesn't have a good attitude	same	opposite

B Look at the pictures. Write 2 adjectives under each picture.

1.

Marisa Tompkins

_____

_____

2.

David Hurst

_____

_____

3.

4.

Simon Land

Grace Vang

_____

_____

C You are an employer and you need to hire someone at your company.

The people in Activity B are applying for the job. Write their names in the order that you want to hire them. Explain why.

	NAME	REASON
1.		
2.		
3.		
4.		

D List 3 good qualities that you have.

1. _____

2. _____

3. _____

An Immigrant Story

LESSON 4

A Read the story. Answer the questions below.

Edwidge Danticat was born in Port-au-Prince, Haiti, in 1969. Her first languages were Creole and French. Her father was a cab driver. When Edwidge was two, her father moved to New York. Her mother moved to New York two years later. Edwidge lived with her aunt in Haiti. She wrote her first story when she was nine years old.

At twelve, she moved to New York to live with her parents. She was very quiet because she had an accent and was different from the other students. Edwidge planned to become a nurse, but she became a writer instead. She published her first book of stories in 1995. Then she wrote other books. She was even on the television show *Oprah*.

1. What is Edwidge Danticat's occupation? _____

2. What is her birthplace? _____

3. Where did she move to? _____

4. What languages did she speak as a child? _____

5. Who did she live with in Haiti? _____

6. Why did she leave Haiti? _____

7. When did she publish her first book? _____

B Complete the sentences about Edwidge Danticat. Use the simple past.

1. When she was two, _____

2. When she was nine, _____

3. When she was twelve, _____

4. When her parents moved to New York, _____

5. In 1995, _____

54

C Complete the sentences about you. Use the simple past.

1. When I was four, _____.

2. When I was ten, _____.

3. When I started school, _____.

4. In 1995, _____.

5. In 2000, _____.

6. _____.

D Write a story about you. Use the simple past. Refer to your sentences in Activity C. Add new ones.

_____

_____

_____

_____

_____

_____

_____

_____

E Read and solve the word problems.

1. Danticat was born in 1969. She moved to New York when she was 12. What year did she

   move to New York? _____

2. Danticat published her first book in 1995. How old was she? _____

3. Frances writes too. It takes her nine months to write a book. If she writes four books,

   how many years will it take? _____

FAMILY

LESSON

Encourage your child to read.

A Check the box if you agree.

☐ Parents should read to their children.

☐ Parents should spend time with their children.

☐ Learning is important for everyone in the family.

☐ Parents should help with homework.

☐ All adult family members should be involved in children's school.

B Read the information. Check *True* or *False* to the questions that follow on page 57.

EducationalDatabase.com

EDUCATIONAL DATABASE.COM

*Search our
online database!*

GO

Help Your Child Succeed In School!

Encourage your child to read.
- Start early, when your child is still a baby.
- Keep books, magazines, and newspapers in the house.
- Show that you like to read. Read as much as you can.
- Get your child help if she or he has a problem with reading.

Talk to your child.
- Talk about school and things you see around you.
- When you go shopping, talk about prices.
- When you are cooking, talk about food and recipes.
- When you watch TV, talk about the programs.
- Pay attention when your child is talking to you.

Help with homework.
- Provide a good place to study.
- Schedule time for homework.
- Turn off the TV and other distractions.
- Tell your child when he or she does a good job.
- Don't worry if your English isn't perfect, you are not doing the homework.

Limit television and video games.
- Don't let your child spend too much time in front of the TV or video screen.
- Watch what your child watches.

Use the library.
- Bring your child to the library often.
- Get your child a library card.
- Ask about special programs at the library.
- Teach your child responsible use of the Internet.

Encourage your child to be responsible.

	True	False
1. You don't need to read to babies because they are too young to understand.	☐	☐
2. You shouldn't let your children watch too much TV. When they do watch, you should watch with them.	☐	☐
3. Children should get their own library cards.	☐	☐
4. If your children don't understand their homework, you should do it for them.	☐	☐
5. If your English isn't very good, you can't help with homework.	☐	☐

C Answer the questions.

1. What are 3 things you can talk about with your child?

_____

2. What are 3 things you should have in your house to read?

_____

3. How can you help with homework?

_____

★ ★

TAKE IT OUTSIDE: Interview a family member, friend, or coworker. Write the answers in the chart.

NUMBER OF CHILDREN	HOW DO YOU HELP YOUR CHILDREN WITH READING?	HOW DO YOU HELP YOUR CHILDREN WITH HOMEWORK?

★ ★

TAKE IT ONLINE: Use the Internet to find information on "how to help children succeed in school." Write 2 new ideas you learn.

1. _____

2. _____

WORK

LESSON

Plan for your future at work.

A Look at the article. Check the things you think will be in the article.

☐ ways to get a promotion

☐ how to make plans

☐ the qualities you need for a better job

☐ the classes you should take

☐ how to fill out an application

☐ what to wear to an interview

☐ the importance of skills and achievements

B Read the article. Check your answers in Activity A.

HOW TO GET A PROMOTION

Do you want a new job or promotion? Follow the steps below and you may get a better position.

1. **Make a plan:** You need to have a plan. What job or position do you want? When do you plan to get the position? What skills or training do you need for the new position?

2. **Do more:** Start doing more work in your job now. Show your supervisor that you are hardworking. Always come to work and meetings on time, and call when you are sick.

3. **Learn more:** A promotion or new job often needs more training or education. Find out what classes or training you can take.

4. **Have a good attitude:** Don't think of your work as just a job. Be pleasant, accept reponsibility, and work hard.

5. **Look the part:** You should dress, speak, and act like the employee in the position you want. Dress neatly, speak politely, and act appropriately.

6. **List your skills and achievements:** Think about your skills and achievements. Can you do anything special? Did you do good work in your last job?

7. **Tell your supervisor:** Your supervisor can help you get a promotion. Tell your supervisor you would like a new position. Ask questions about the position. Find out what you need to do.

C Read the article again. Complete the sentences.

1. If you want a promotion, you should tell _____.

2. You need to show that you are _____.

3. Always come to work _____.

4. If you are sick, you should _____.

5. Find out _____ to get a promotion.

D Complete the sentences about you.

1. If I want to get a promotion, I should learn _____.

2. If I want to get a better job, I should be _____ and

_____.

3. If I want my supervisor to help me, I should _____.

★ ★

TAKE IT OUTSIDE: Interview a family member, friend, or coworker. Write the answers.

1. Did you get a raise or a promotion in your job? _____

2. Why? _____

3. What do you think someone should do to get a promotion?

_____

_____

★ ★

REVIEW

LESSON

Practice Test

DIRECTIONS: Choose the best answer. Use the Answer Sheet.

1. If I want to graduate from a university, I should:
   A. get a job
   B. get married
   C. study hard
   D. be a good parent

2. If she wants to be a good parent, she should:
   A. let her children watch a lot of TV
   B. read to her children
   C. work a lot
   D. start a business

3. Cathy wants a promotion. What can she do?
   A. take a class
   B. get married
   C. have children
   D. be lazy

4. Five hundred and nineteen students registered for Adult ESL classes this semester. There are 25 students in a class. How many classes do they need?
   A. 20
   B. 25
   C. 50
   D. 21

5. Patty works in an office. She is writing letters. She can write 10 letters in an hour. How many letters can she write in one day if she works 8 hours?
   A. 80
   B. 10
   C. 40
   D. 160

ANSWER SHEET				
1	A	B	C	D
2	A	B	C	D
3	A	B	C	D
4	A	B	C	D
5	A	B	C	D
6	A	B	C	D
7	A	B	C	D
8	A	B	C	D
9	A	B	C	D
10	A	B	C	D

DIRECTIONS: Look at the schedule to answer the next 5 questions. Use the Answer Sheet on page 60.

Fall Semester Schedule

Classes Begin (GED, Adult High School, Adult ESL)	Mon., Aug. 18
Classes Begin (academic programs)	Sat., Aug. 23
Labor Day Holiday	Mon., Sept. 7
Fall Break — no classes	Mon., Oct. 13 — Tues., Oct. 14
Thanksgiving Holiday	Thurs., Nov. 27 — Fri., Nov. 28
Final Exam Period	Mon., Dec. 8 — Fri., Dec. 12
Semester Ends	Sat., Dec. 13
Graduation	Sun., Dec. 14
Winter Holidays	Mon., Dec. 15 — Wed., Dec. 31
New Year's Holiday	Thurs., Jan. 1 — Fri., Jan. 2

6. What date do GED classes begin?

   A. Monday

   B. August 18

   C. Saturday

   D. August 23

7. What date do academic classes begin?

   A. Monday

   B. August 18

   C. Saturday

   D. August 23

8. When is graduation?

   A. Dec. 8

   B. Dec. 12

   C. Dec. 13

   D. Dec. 14

9. How many days is fall break?

   A. one

   B. two

   C. three

   D. four

10. What happens on September 7?

   A. classes begin

   B. fall break

   C. graduation

   D. Labor Day holiday

HOW DID YOU DO? Count the number of correct answers on your answer sheet. Record this number in the bar graph on the inside back cover.

LESSON 1

Do you have a heavy coat?

A Write the words under the pictures.

| blender | boots | bucket | coat | mop | vacuum |

1. _____

& _____

2. _____

3. _____

4. _____

5. _____

B Write 1 sentence about each picture.

1. _____

2. _____

3. _____

4. _____

5. _____

C Match the actions and the things.

Actions	Things
1. _____ What can you use to clean the floor?	a. a jacket
2. _____ What can you use to make juice?	b. a mop
3. _____ What can you wear to stay warm?	c. a can opener
4. _____ What can you use to open cans?	d. a toaster
5. _____ What can you use to wash glasses?	e. a blender
6. _____ What can you use to toast bread?	f. dish soap

D Complete the sentences with a comparative form of the adjective in parentheses.

1. Susana feels _____ (good) today than yesterday.

2. The brown coat is _____ (nice) than the blue one.

3. This toaster is _____ (expensive) than that one.

4. The weather is _____ (bad) this year.

5. Our new house is _____ (big) than our old one.

6. A can opener is _____ (useful) than a blender.

comparatives

E Answer the questions about you.

1. Is your teacher nicer than your classmates? _____

_____

2. Is your home now bigger than your home 10 years ago? _____

_____

3. Is the weather today better than yesterday? _____

_____

4. Are your food expenses cheaper than your transportation expenses? _____

_____

LESSON 2

Where do you buy shoes?

A Find these words in the puzzle. Circle them.

appliance	jewelry
break	mall
business	mop
can opener	peeler
carry	push
coat	sale
furniture	stroller

```
w  a  p  p  l  i  a  n  c  e
p  n  e  u  o  b  r  e  a  k
u  j  e  w  e  l  r  y  n  t
s  i  l  t  e  c  h  o  o  w
h  r  e  v  u  e  m  o  p  e
c  a  r  r  y  s  a  l  e  r
o  d  z  e  q  c  l  a  n  p
a  v  s  t  r  o  l  l  e  r
t  f  u  r  n  i  t  u  r  e
u  n  b  u  s  i  n  e  s  s
```

B Match the questions and answers.

Questions

1. Where do you buy shoes?
2. Do you have a coffeemaker?
3. Is May's better than Arches?
4. Where can you buy a blender?
5. What did you buy at Ben's furniture store?
6. Was it on sale?

Answers

a. Yes. It was cheaper than last week.
b. I think so. It's cheaper.
c. At Sam's appliance store.
d. I like May's department store.
e. Two chairs.
f. No, I don't. I need one.

C Write 3 things you can buy at each place.

AN APPLIANCE STORE	A FURNITURE STORE	A DEPARTMENT STORE

D Look at the mall directory. Check *yes* or *no* to the statements below.

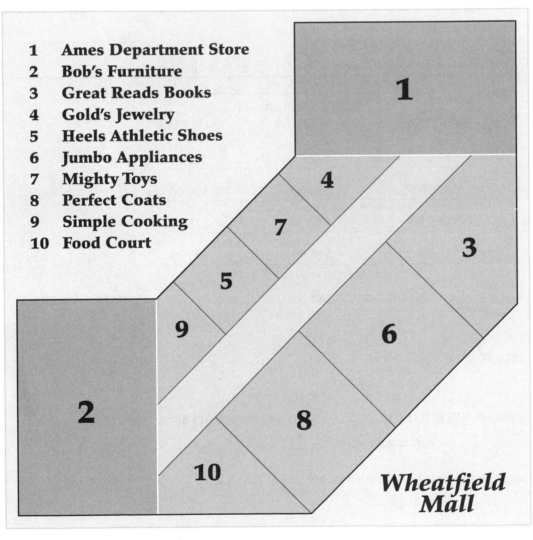

1   Ames Department Store
2   Bob's Furniture
3   Great Reads Books
4   Gold's Jewelry
5   Heels Athletic Shoes
6   Jumbo Appliances
7   Mighty Toys
8   Perfect Coats
9   Simple Cooking
10 Food Court

Wheatfield Mall

1. The jewelry store is next to the bookstore.	☐ yes	☐ no
2. The food court is across from Simple Cooking.	☐ yes	☐ no
3. The toy store is between the jewelry store and the appliance store.	☐ yes	☐ no
4. Bob's Furniture is near the food court.	☐ yes	☐ no
5. You can buy athletic shoes across from the coat store.	☐ yes	☐ no
6. You can buy a can opener at store 3.	☐ yes	☐ no

3
LESSON

I saved seven dollars.

A Put the conversation in order. Number the sentences from first (1) to last (5).

_1_ I think so. I saved twelve dollars.

_____ Yes. I got one at Barb's.

_____ That's a good deal.

_____ Really? Did you get a good deal?

_____ Did you get a new blender?

B Look at the price comparison chart. Circle the correct answer below.

ITEM	AL'S SUPERSTORE	BOB'S DISCOUNT HOUSE	BEST PRICE
toaster	$29.00	$32.99	$30.89
blender	$21.99	$19.00	$25.00
electric can opener	$14.99	$16.00	$13.99
electric toothbrush	$19.99	$18.00	$20.00

1. If you are buying a blender, Bob's Discount House is _cheaper_ than Al's Superstore.
   A. cheaper   B. more expensive

2. If you want to get a toaster, Best Price is _more expensive_ than Al's Superstore.
   A. cheaper   B. more expensive

3. Electric can openers are _cheaper_ than blenders at Al's Superstore.
   A. cheaper   B. more expensive

4. At Bob's Discount House, electric toothbrushes are _18.00_ .
   A. $16.00   B. $18.00

5. Best Price has a good deal on _electric can openers._
   A. electric can openers   B. electric toothbrushes

C Write the amounts.

1. 50% of $100 = $50.00
2. 50% of $500 =   250.00
3. 10% of $500 =   50.00
4. 20% of $200 =   40.00
5. 10% of $35 =   3.50
6. 80% of $320 =   256.00

D Look at the chart in Activity B. Answer the questions.

1. Electric can openers are on sale at Bob's Discount House.
   They are 20% off. What price are they on sale?   12.00

2. Blenders are 40% off at Best Price. What is the sale price?   15.00

3. Al's Superstore is having a sale on toasters.
   They're 10% off. What's the sale price?   26.10

4. Electric toothbrushes are going on sale tomorrow at Best Price.
   They are going to be 25% off. How much are they going to cost tomorrow?   _____

5. If blenders are 10% off at Best Price, are they cheaper
   than at Bob's Discount House?   _____

E Complete the chart.

WHAT 3 THINGS DO YOU NEED TO BUY SOON?	WHAT DO YOU THINK IS A GOOD PRICE FOR EACH ITEM?	WHERE ARE YOU GOING TO SHOP?

A Shopper's Calendar

A Read the magazine article. Circle the words that are new to you.

break/broken	recycle	repair	replace
technology	trade association	reputation	

Is it time for a new one?

The toaster or computer is a couple of years old, and there isn't a warranty. Should you fix it or forget it? When you break an appliance or electronic product, you may want to buy a newer one if it has better technology, or if the repair is more than half the cost of a new one.

Buy a new one? Sometimes new products are much cheaper than they used to be, making them a better deal. Also replacing a broken small appliance (e.g., a toaster) can be cheaper than making a repair. Also, it can be difficult to find parts for the old model.

Fix it? Make sure the product is really broken. Sometimes you can go to the website for the product and find out how to solve small problems. If you decide to repair the item, call the company. Sometimes they will replace the item for free. If you take the item to a repair shop, make sure the repairer belongs to a trade association or has a good reputation. Call the Better Business Bureau if you have a problem with a repair.

Throw it away? Don't throw away products that can cause problems, including computer parts and batteries. Try to recycle. Many organizations and schools are happy to take computers and appliances.

B Check *yes* or *no*.

1. It's always cheaper to repair a broken appliance.   ☐ yes   ☐ no

2. You should buy a new one if the repair is expensive.   ☐ yes   ☐ no

3. Sometimes a company will give you a new item.   ☐ yes   ☐ no

4. You should throw away old computers.   ☐ yes   ☐ no

5. Companies sometimes have websites that give information on problems.   ☐ yes   ☐ no

C Circle the correct answer.

1. When is it a good idea to repair a broken appliance?

   A. When the repair is cheap.

   B. When the repair is expensive.

2. What is one problem with repairs?

   A. They are always more expensive than getting a new one.

   B. Sometimes parts are hard to find.

3. Can you throw away the old item?

   A. You can throw some things away, but not others.

   B. Yes, always.

4. What should you do with old computers?

   A. Throw them away.

   B. Recycle them.

5. What should you do if you have a problem with a repairer?

   A. Buy a new appliance.

   B. Call the Better Business Bureau.

D Answer the questions about you. Check the correct box.

WHEN SOMETHING IS BROKEN, HOW OFTEN DO YOU	ALWAYS	SOMETIMES	NEVER
try to fix it?			
ask someone you know to fix it?			
take it back to the store?			
call the company?			
buy a replacement (a new one)?			
throw it away?			

E Write 2 sentences about something that broke and what you did.

_____

_____

_____

WORK

LESSON

What do you wear to work?

A Look at the website. Check the items you see.

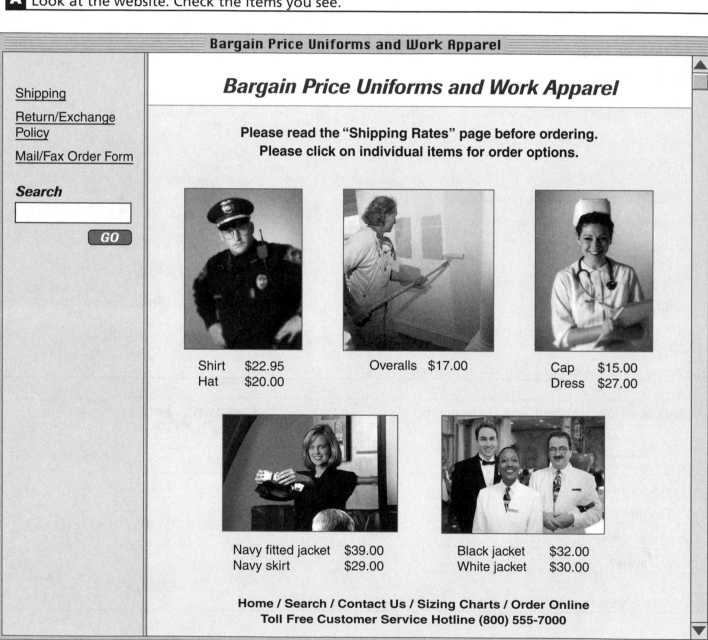

Bargain Price Uniforms and Work Apparel

Bargain Price Uniforms and Work Apparel

Please read the "Shipping Rates" page before ordering.
Please click on individual items for order options.

Shipping

Return/Exchange Policy

Mail/Fax Order Form

Search

GO

Shirt	$22.95
Hat	$20.00

Overalls $17.00

Cap	$15.00
Dress	$27.00

Navy fitted jacket	$39.00
Navy skirt	$29.00

Black jacket	$32.00
White jacket	$30.00

Home / Search / Contact Us / Sizing Charts / Order Online
Toll Free Customer Service Hotline (800) 555-7000

❑ Nurse's cap

❑ Police officer's shirt

❑ Police officer's pants

❑ Painter's overalls

❑ Doctor's coat

❑ Waiter's jacket

❑ Flight attendant's jacket

B Read the website. Write the prices next to the items.

1. overalls _____

2. navy flight attendant's jacket _____

3. white dress _____

4. police officer's hat _____

5. black jacket _____

C Answer the questions.

1. What are 2 things a nurse might wear to work?

_____

2. Who wears a uniform jacket to work?

_____

3. What occupations often have white uniforms?

_____

★ ★

TAKE IT OUTSIDE: Interview a friend, family member, or coworker. Write the answers.

1. What do you wear to work?_____

2. Where do you buy your work clothes? _____

3. How much money do you spend on work clothes each year? _____

★ ★

 TAKE IT ONLINE: Research the prices for one kind of uniform. Use the Internet to search for your item (painting overalls, nurse's cap, etc.) and find the best prices.

Sign up for a gift registry.

A Read the article. Write a definition for *gift registry* below.

Gift Registries

Do you have a special occasion coming up soon? Maybe you're having a baby, getting married, or moving to a new house?

Help your friends and family shop for your gifts. Register with a department store's gift registry. Go to the store and talk to a salesclerk. Tell them you want to sign up for their registry. They will give you a form and you can check the things you want. When your friends and family go to the store, they can get the list. The store checks things off on the list when people buy them for you. That way you don't get too many of anything on the list. Many stores will let you register online, too.

Gift registries can make everyone happy. You get gifts you like. Your friends and family don't have to spend so much time shopping.

A gift registry is _____

_____

B Complete the sentences.

1. Some special occasions are _____,

   _____ or _____.

2. You can sign up for a gift registry in two ways: go to _____ or

   register _____.

3. You use a form and _____ the things you want.

4. One advantage of a gift registry is _____.

5. Friends and family may like gift registries because _____.

C Read the sentences below. Write them in the correct place in the chart.

You can receive a gift you really want.

You have to buy what's on the list.

It is not always easy to go to the store.

You have to wait a long time to talk to a salesclerk and complete the forms.

Shopping for a gift is faster.

You won't get five of the same thing.

REASONS GIFT REGISTRIES ARE A GOOD IDEA	REASONS GIFT REGISTRIES ARE A BAD IDEA

D Answer the questions.

1. What special occasions do you have coming up soon?

   _____

2. Do you think a gift registry is a good idea? Why or why not?

   _____

★ ★

TAKE IT OUTSIDE: Interview 2 people. Write the answers.

DO YOU LIKE GIFT REGISTRIES?	WHY OR WHY NOT?

★ ★

TAKE IT ONLINE: Search the Internet for gift registries. Find out if a department store that you like has an online gift registry.

Practice Test

DIRECTIONS: Look at the mall directory to answer the next 5 questions. Use the Answer Sheet.

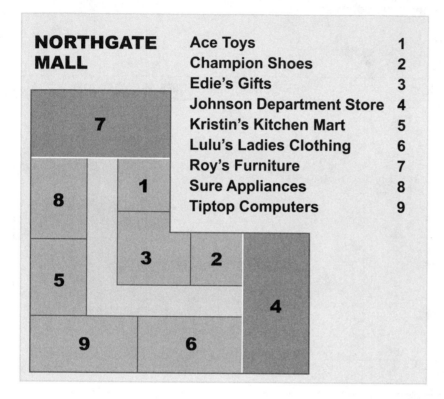

NORTHGATE MALL

Ace Toys	1
Champion Shoes	2
Edie's Gifts	3
Johnson Department Store	4
Kristin's Kitchen Mart	5
Lulu's Ladies Clothing	6
Roy's Furniture	7
Sure Appliances	8
Tiptop Computers	9

ANSWER SHEET

	A	B	C	D
1	A	B	C	D
2	A	B	C	D
3	A	B	C	D
4	A	B	C	D
5	A	B	C	D
6	A	B	C	D
7	A	B	C	D
8	A	B	C	D
9	A	B	C	D
10	A	B	C	D

1. Ace Toys is across from:

   A. Champion shoes

   B. Edie's Gifts

   C. Sure Appliances

   D. Tiptop Computers

2. Where is Edie's Gifts?

   A. between Ace Toys and Champion Shoes

   B. across from Johnson Department Store

   C. next to Lulu's Ladies Clothing

   D. behind Sure Appliances

3. What store is across from 6?

   A. Lulu's Ladies Clothing

   B. Champion Shoes

   C. Ace Toys

   D. Roy's Furniture

4. Where can you buy a toaster?

   A. Edie's Gifts

   B. Champion Shoes

   C. Sure Appliances

   D. Roy's Furniture

5. Where can you buy a desk?

   A. Kristin's Kitchen Mart

   B. Champion Shoes

   C. Ace Toys

   D. Roy's Furniture

DIRECTIONS: Look at the ad to answer the next 5 questions. Use the Answer Sheet on page 74.

6. What is the sale price of the toasters?

   A. $30.00

   B. $24.99

   C. $120.00

   D. $99.99

7. What is the regular price of vacuums?

   A. $30.00

   B. $24.99

   C. $120.00

   D. $99.99

8. If the regular price of a coffeemaker is $40, what is the sale price?

   A. $24.99

   B. $99.99

   C. $20.00

   D. $10.00

9. What is the sale price of a blender that is regularly $20?

   A. $20.00

   B. $10.00

   C. $5.00

   D. $4.00

10. How much money do you save when you buy a vacuum on sale?

   A. $20.01

   B. $5.01

   C. 50%

   D. 80%

HOW DID YOU DO? Count the number of correct answers on your answer sheet. Record this number in the bar graph on the inside back cover.

Spotlight: Grammar

COMPARATIVE FORMS OF ADJECTIVES	
One-Syllable Adjectives	**Two-Syllable Adjectives**
• Add -*er* to most one-syllable adjectives. EXAMPLES: old/older tall/taller • For one-syllable adjectives that end in a single vowel and a consonant, double the consonant and add -*er*. EXAMPLES: hot/hotter fat/fatter	• For two-syllable adjectives that end in -*y*, change the -*y* to -*i* and add -*er*. EXAMPLE: happy/happier • Use the word "more" with most two-syllable adjectives. EXAMPLE: beautiful/more beautiful

Irregular Adjectives
good/better
bad/worse
far/farther

A Look at the photos. Complete the sentences with the comparative form of the adjectives in parentheses.

Grace

Peter

1. Grace is _____ (pretty) than Peter.

2. Peter is _____ (young) than Grace.

3. Grace is _____ (happy) than Peter.

4. Peter's hair is _____ (short) than Grace's hair.

5. Grace has _____ (long) hair than Peter does.

B Write 3 sentences comparing Peter and Grace using the adjectives *sad, old* and *beautiful.*

1. _____

2. _____

3. _____

SUPERLATIVE FORMS OF ADJECTIVES	
One-Syllable Adjectives	**Two-Syllable Adjectives**

One-Syllable Adjectives

- Add -*est* to most one-syllable adjectives.
  EXAMPLE: cheap/the cheapest

- For one-syllable adjectives that end in a single vowel and a consonant, double the consonant and add -*est*.
  EXAMPLE: hot/the hottest

Two-Syllable Adjectives

- For two-syllable adjectives that end in -*y*, change the -*y* to -*i* and add -*est*.
  EXAMPLE: happy/the happiest

- Use the word "most" with most adjectives with two or more syllables.
  EXAMPLE: beautiful/the most beautiful

Irregular Adjectives
good/the best
bad/the worst
far/the farthest

C Complete the sentences. Use *the* and the superlative form of the adjectives in parentheses.

1. _____*oldest*_____ American is about 113 years old. (old)   *sobre algo*

2. Muhammad Ali is perhaps _____ fighter. (famous)

3. _____ buildings in the world are in Kuala Lumpur. (tall)

4. The Nile is _____ river in the world. (long)

5. Russia is _____ country. (large)

6. A cheetah can run 46 miles per hour. It is _____ animal. (fast)

7. Cuba is home to _____ bird in the world. (small)

8. People thought Helen of Troy was _____ woman of that time. (beautiful)

9. Mauna Loa may be _____ mountain. (big)

10. _____ place on earth is El Azizia, a desert in Libya. (hot)

D Answer the questions.

1. Who is the youngest person in your family?

   _____

2. What is the best kind of food?

   _____

3. What is the worst thing that happened last year?

   _____

Did you eat any fish yesterday?

A Write the words under the pictures.

1.

red meat

2.

_____

3.

_____

4.

_____

5.

_____

6.

_____

B List the foods above in order of your preference (*1* is the food you like best).

1. _____

2. _____

3. _____

4. _____

5. _____

6. _____

C Complete the questions. Write *How much* or *How many.*

1. _____ red meat did you eat last week?

2. _____ eggs do you eat every week?

3. _____ coffee do you drink every day?

4. _____ soft drinks did you drink yesterday?

5. _____ oil should you eat a day?

how much and *how many*

D Answer the questions in Activity C.

1. _____

2. _____

3. _____

4. _____

5. _____

E Compare what you should eat and what you like to eat. Write 3 foods in each category.

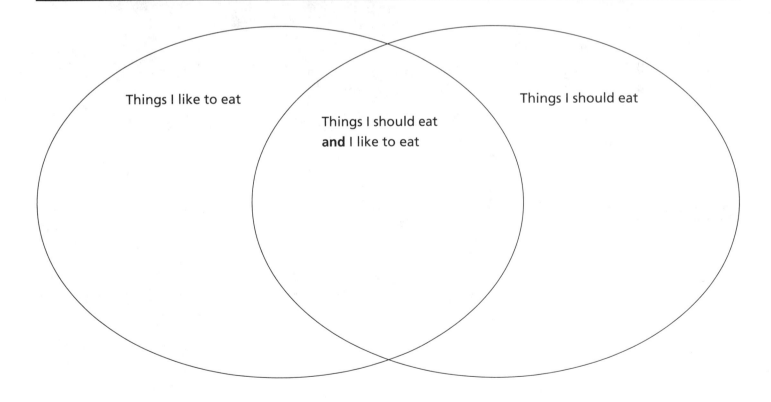

Things I like to eat

Things I should eat
and I like to eat

Things I should eat

Can you bring me a menu, please?

A Look at the picture. Check the things you see.

- ❏ a waiter
- ❏ customers
- ❏ a table
- ❏ a booth
- ❏ a counter
- ❏ a plate
- ❏ soft drinks
- ❏ coffee
- ❏ bread
- ❏ eggs
- ❏ fish
- ❏ a napkin
- ❏ pouring
- ❏ taking an order
- ❏ clearing
- ❏ serving
- ❏ eating
- ❏ smiling

B Write 3 sentences about the picture.

1. _____

2. _____

3. _____

C Match the questions and answers.

Questions

1. Can I help you?
2. Can you bring us some water?
3. How much was the check?
4. Did you eat your bread?
5. Would you like more coffee?
6. How many eggs would you like?

Answers

a. Yes. I'll get some right away.
b. No, I didn't.
c. Yes, please. A little more.
d. Yes. I'd like some milk, please.
e. Three.
f. About $20.

D Complete the sentences.

1. A _____ takes your order.

2. You usually eat cereal in a _____, not a plate.

3. If you pour a drink too fast, you might _____ it.

4. A _____ is a list of the food you can order.

5. Use a _____ to clean your face after you eat.

E Answer the questions about you. Write complete sentences.

1. How often do you eat in a restaurant?

   _____

2. Do you like booths or tables better?

   _____

3. Can you read most menus?

   _____

4. The last time you went to a restaurant, did a hostess take you to your seat?

   _____

5. Do you usually understand the waiter?

   _____

Root Beer

3 LESSON Are you ready to order?

A Complete the sentences.

ACROSS

1. Another name for drinks is _beverager_.
4. Many people like _Ice Cream_. It is very cold and sweet. You can eat it for dessert.
5. A waiter often brings food to the table on a _tray_.
6. You usually eat _desserts_ after a meal. It is usually something sweet, like cake.
8. A _main dish_ is the important part of the meal. Many people in the United States eat red meat, poultry, or fish as the _main dishe_.

DOWN

2. _Vegetables_ are good for you. They include carrots, green beans, and spinach.
3. You eat an _Appetizer_ before your meal.
7. Some people eat _main dish_ before the meal. Some people eat it with the meal. Some people eat it after the meal. It is usually made with lettuce and other vegetables.

B Write the words in the crossword puzzle.

¹B	E	²V	E	R	³A	G	E	R		
		E			P					
		G			P					
⁴I	C	e	C	r	e	a	m			
		T			T					
⁵T	R	A	Y		I					
		B			Z					
		L		⁶d	e	s	⁷s	c	t	s
		E			r		a			
		S					L			
							A			
				⁸m	a	i	n	D	i	s	h

C Put the conversation in order. Number the sentences from first (1) to last (6).

_2_ Yes. I'd like a small garden salad and a hamburger.

_5_ Large or small?

_3_ Do you want something to drink with your hamburger?

_1_ Are you ready to order?

_4_ Yes. I'd like some milk, please.

_6_ Large, please.

D Look at the menu. Answer the questions.

1. What do you get with a grilled chicken sandwich?

   _____

2. How much is a tuna sandwich?

   _____

3. You order the fresh fruit plate and a hamburger.

   How much is it?

   _____

4. How can you find out what kind of cake is for dessert?

   _____

5. What do you get with the fish of the day?

   _____

La Dee Da's

LUNCH MENU

Appetizers

Chips and dip	$3.95
Fresh fruit plate	$4.25

Sandwiches

(served with chips and pickle)

Grilled chicken	$4.95
Hamburger	$5.25
Tuna	$4.25

Main Dishes

(served with salad and potato)

Roasted half chicken	$6.95
Fish of the day	$8.50

Desserts

Ice cream, cake, or pie. Ask your waiter for today's choices.

E Write the amounts.

1. 15% tip on $10.00 = _____

2. 20% tip on $32.00 = _____

3. 5% tax on $15.00 = _____

4. 7% tax on $8.00 = _____

83

Favorite Recipes

A Write 1 sentence for each picture. Tell what the cook is doing. Use a word from the box.

| bake | cut up | fry | heat | slice |

1. The cook is _____

   _____.

2. _____

   _____.

3. _____

   _____.

4. _____

   _____.

5. _____

   _____.

B Match the quantity words and the food.

Quantity Words   **Food**

1. _____ 3 slices   a. of coffee
2. _____ 5 cups   b. of bread
3. _____ 2 pieces   c. of milk
4. _____ 1 glass   d. of shrimp
5. _____ 2 bowls   e. of chicken
6. _____ 12 pounds   f. of soup

C Answer the questions about you. Use quantity words.

1. What did you drink yesterday?

_____

2. How much red meat do you usually eat each week?

_____

3. What did you eat for dinner last night?

_____

D Read the recipe. Write the amounts.

Almond Balls (cookies)

1 cup butter (soft)   2 tsp. vanilla
1/2 cup sugar   2 cups flour
2 tsp. water   1/2 cup chopped nuts
powdered sugar for rolling

Mix the butter, sugar, water, and vanilla. Then add the flour and nuts. Mix again. Put in the refrigerator until firm. Form balls 1" wide. Bake at 325° for 15 minutes. Cool. Roll in powdered sugar.

To make these cookies, you will mix

_____ of butter,

_____ of sugar,

_____ of water, and

_____ of vanilla in a bowl.

Then you add _____ of flour

and _____ of nuts. Mix

again.

FAMILY

LESSON

Unit 6: Food

What is your favorite holiday?

A Look at the picture and the title of the story. Check what you know.

- ☑ The man is happy.
- ❑ The man is sad.
- ❑ His family is from China.
- ☑ His family is from Cuba.
- ☑ The story is about family.
- ❑ The story is about work.

Cuban Family Traditions

Cubans have a lot of traditions. One of my favorite times is Christmas Eve. Everyone in the family gets together and eats dinner. My father roasts a whole pig. He kills it himself on December 23. My mother cooks the best black beans and rice you can think of. We drink strong Cuban coffee. Everyone sits in the living room and tells stories about the old days. I love Christmas Eve.

Gabriel Herrera

B Read the story. Circle the correct answer.

1. What holiday is Gabriel talking about?
   A. New Year's   B. Memorial Day   c. Christmas Eve

2. What kind of meat do they eat?
   A. roast pig   B. roast chicken   c. fish

3. What other food do they eat?
   A. rice and salad   B. black beans and rice   c. soup

4. What do they drink?
   A. water   B. coffee   c. milk

5. What does the family like to do in the living room?
   A. watch TV   B. listen to music   c. tell stories

86

C Answer the questions about you.

1. What is your favorite holiday? _New Years and Chrismas_
2. What foods do you eat then? _Chicken black beans and Turkey_
3. What was your favorite food as a child? _____

D Write a story about a family tradition. Use Gabriel's story as a model.

In Mexico we have a lot of traditions. My favorite times is New Years What is gets together and eats dinner. My mother and gramather cooks together the best Pozole you can think of. We drink light ponche. Everyone They are of outdisc breaking pinatas and tells stories old Years I love end to of Years.

* *

TAKE IT OUTSIDE: Interview a family member, friend, or coworker. Complete the chart.

WHAT WAS YOUR FAVORITE FAMILY HOLIDAY AS A CHILD?	WHAT DID YOU EAT?	WHAT DID YOU DO?

* *

TAKE IT ONLINE: Search the Internet for "food traditions" + a nationality that interests you. Bring in information to share with the class.

What kind of event is it?

A Read the information about planning an event for work. Complete the sentences below.

What you need to find out first

Before you talk to your caterer about the food, answer these questions.

1. How many people will attend the event?

2. What kind of event is it? Will you serve dinner?

3. If you are serving appetizers, do you want light, medium, or heavy appetizers
(light=snack, medium=possible meal, heavy=a meal)?

4. What types of beverages? Hot or cold?

5. Is it a sit-down meal? Do you want square or round tables?

7. Are there any colors you prefer?

8. Do you need flowers or balloons?

1. A _____ caterer _____ is someone who takes care of the food for an event.

2. You need to know how many _____ will attend.

3. You should decide if you want hot or cold _____.

4. There are three types of _____: light, medium, and heavy.

5. You can get square or round _____.

6. You need to decide if you want _____ or

_____ for the room.

B Answer the questions about you.

1. What was the last special work event you went to?

_____

2. What kind of food did they have?

_____

C Read the form. Match the questions and answers below.

Big City Caterers

Welcome to Big City Caterers Online Registration

First name:	Linda	Last name:	Muhammad
Date of event:	3/12/2007	Location:	Bainbridge Hall
Set up time:	3:30 p.m.	Time of event:	6:00 p.m.
Email address:	lmuhammad@hamiltonpress.com	Telephone:	(617)555-9002

Comments/questions:

Company awards banquet. Sit-down dinner with round tables. Servers to pass light appetizers. Cold beverages with the meal, hot beverages after the meal.

Questions	Answers
1. What is Linda's last name?	a. (617) 555-9002
2. Where is the event?	b. Muhammad
3. What is the event?	c. 6 o'clock
4. What time does the event begin?	d. company awards banquet
5. What is Linda's phone number?	e. Bainbridge Hall

★★★

TAKE IT OUTSIDE: Interview a family member, friend, or coworker. Ask about a future or past event. Complete the form.

Big City Caterers

Welcome to Big City Caterers Online Registration

First name:		Last name:	
Date of event:		Location:	
Set up time:		Time of event:	
Email address:		Telephone:	

Comments/questions:

★★★

REVIEW

LESSON

Practice Test

DIRECTIONS: Look at the food label to answer the next 5 questions. Use the Answer Sheet.

INGREDIENTS: CORN MEAL, WHOLE OATS, OIL, SUGAR, SALT, CALCIUM CARBONATE, MODIFIED CORN STARCH, WHEAT STARCH

ANSWER SHEET

	A	B	C	D
1	A	B	C	D
2	A	B	C	D
3	A	B	C	D
4	A	B	C	D
5	A	B	C	D
6	A	B	C	D
7	A	B	C	D
8	A	B	C	D
9	A	B	C	D
10	A	B	C	D

1. What kind of food is this?

   A. poultry

   B. rice

   C. cereal

   D. corn

2. Which ingredient is found in the largest amount?

   A. corn meal

   B. corn starch

   C. wheat starch

   D. salt

3. Which ingredient is found in the smallest amount?

   A. corn meal

   B. corn starch

   C. wheat starch

   D. salt

4. Which ingredient is NOT found in this product?

   A. oats

   B. oil

   C. butter

   D. salt

5. Is there more calcium carbonate, wheat starch, sugar, or oil?

   A. calcium carbonate

   B. wheat starch

   C. sugar

   D. oil

DIRECTIONS: Look at the menu to answer the next 5 questions. Use the Answer Sheet on page 90.

MENU

Appetizers

Shrimp	$6.95
Fruit plate	$4.50
Chips and dip	$4.25

Soups and Salads

Green side salad	$3.50
Caesar salad	$6.95
Onion soup	$3.00
Chicken soup	$3.50

Sides

Baked potatoes, vegetables and rice can be added for $2.00 each.

Main Dishes

(includes soup or salad, bread, potato, vegetable)

Steak	$16.00
Roast chicken	$9.50
Fish of the day	market price
Hamburger	$8.00

Beverages

Coffee, tea	$1.50
Milk	$2.00
Soft drinks	$1.75

6. What is the cheapest appetizer?

   A. chips and dip

   B. green side salad

   C. fruit plate

   D. onion soup

7. You order roast chicken with a salad and a potato. How much do you pay for them?

   A. $12.00

   B. $9.50

   C. $13.00

   D. $16.00

8. What kind of order is milk?

   A. appetizer

   B. soup

   C. beverage

   D. main dish

9. What is the cheapest item on the menu?

   A. onion soup

   B. coffee

   C. rice

   D. a soft drink

10. What is the most expensive item on the menu?

   A. roast chicken

   B. steak

   C. caesar salad

   D. shrimp

HOW DID YOU DO? Count the number of correct answers on your answer sheet. Record this number in the bar graph on the inside back cover.

She's Juan's grandmother.

A Complete the sentences.

ACROSS

1. I am married to your sister. I am your _____.
3. I am your brother's daughter. I am your _____.
6. I am going to marry your brother soon. I am your brother's _____.
7. I am your father's brother. I am your _____.
9. We do things together. You can talk to me anytime. I am your _____.
10. I supervise you at work. I am your _____.
11. We are your mother's parents. We are your _____.

DOWN

2. I own the place where you live. I am your _____.
3. I am your sister's son. I am your _____.
4. We work at the same place. I am your _____.
5. We are your mother and father. We are your _____.
8. I live next to you. I am your _____.

B Write the words in the crossword puzzle.

C Look at the family tree diagram. Answer the questions below.

whose/who's

female ◯   male ☐

1. Who's Ivan's sister?   _____

2. Whose wife is Maria?   _____

3. Who's Scott's grandfather?   _____

4. Whose niece is Anita?   _____

5. Whose husband is Jerome?   _____

D Answer the questions about you.

1. Where do your parents live?   _____

2. How many uncles do you have?   _____

3. Whose son or daughter are you?   _____

4. Are your neighbors friendly?   _____

5. Who's your best friend?   _____

6. Who was your favorite boss?   _____

7. Who's your father?   _____

8. Whose parent are you?   _____

9. Whose neighbor are you?   _____

Who's dancing with Tito?

A Write the words under the pictures.

| dance | kiss | make a toast | shake hands |

1.

_____

2.

_____

3.

_____

4.

_____

B Write 1 sentence about each picture. Use the words from Activity A.

1. _____

2. _____

3. _____

4. _____

C Look at the pictures on page 94 again. Circle the correct answer.

whose/who's

1. Who's dancing with Angela?

   A. That's her teacher.   B. Yes, it is.

2. Whose mother is that?

   A. The woman on the right.   B. The little girl's.

3. Who's the new employee?

   A. The one on the left. Mike Hawes.   B. I think so.

4. Whose company is it?

   A. It belongs to Ed Yates.   B. A coworker's.

5. Who's making the toast?

   A. No. I haven't met her.   B. My father.

D Write the words in the correct order.

1. the mother / That's / of the groom /.

   _____

2. with / Who's / your father /dancing / ?

   _____

3. in this picture / are you hugging / mother / Whose / ?

   _____

4. fiancée / is / My brother's / from China /.

   _____

5. Lalo / at my wedding / a toast / made /.

   _____

3
LESSON

Sorry I'm late.

A Read the conversations. Identify the actions.

1. A: Hi, Fernanda. How's it going?

   B: Terrible. I had a fight with Jack. Do you think I should call him?

2. A: You missed the meeting. Where were you?

   B: I'm so sorry. I completely forgot.

3. A: This meal is delicious.

   B: Thank you. I'm glad you like it.

4. A: Did you read the report?

   B: Yes. You're going to have to write it again. It's not very good.

5. A: I really like that lab instructor.

   B: Really? I think she's a little disorganized.

6. A: You need to do your homework before you can watch TV.

   B: No. I don't want to do my homework.

1. _____ask for advice_____

2. _____apologize_____

3. _____complimet_____

4. _____criticize_____

5. _____disagree_____

6. _____talk back_____

B Read the sentences. Underline *should* or *shouldn't*.

1. You (should / shouldn't) ask for advice when you have a problem.

2. You (should / shouldn't) disagree with your friends.

3. You (should / shouldn't) talk back to your parents.

4. You (should / shouldn't) criticize your boss.

5. You (should / shouldn't) yell at your wife or husband.

6. You (should / shouldn't) compliment a friend.

7. You (should / shouldn't) apologize if you are late to work.

C Complete the flow chart with sentences from the box.

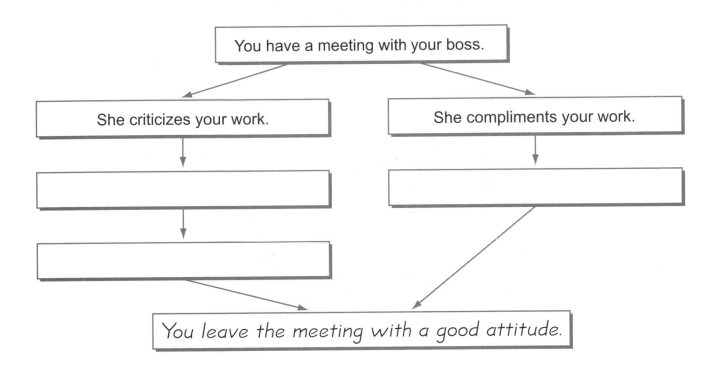

You leave the meeting with a good attitude.   You thank your boss.
You ask for advice on how to do a better job.   You apologize.

You have a meeting with your boss.

She criticizes your work.   She compliments your work.

You leave the meeting with a good attitude.

D Complete the sentences. Circle the best answer.

1. People usually _____ for a wedding.
   A. dress   B. dress up

2. I _____ vegetables in my garden.
   A. grow   B. grow up

3. Children shouldn't _____ to their teachers.
   A. talk   B. talk back

4. You can _____ books from the library.
   A. check   B. check out

5. Go to Bank Street. _____ left and go one block.
   A. Turn   B. Turn down

Family Traditions

LESSON 4

A Look at the picture. Answer the questions below.

1. How many people do you see? _____

2. What kind of party is it? _____

3. Whose party is it? _____

4. How are the people related? _____

5. What are they doing? _____

B Write 5 sentences about the picture. Use ideas from Activity A.

_____

_____

_____

_____

_____

98

C Read the story. Complete the sentences below.

Moon Yuet

Chinese families often celebrate a baby's first month, or Moon Yuet. Long ago, many babies did not live through the first month. So families had a party when the baby was one month old. They believe that the spirits of family ancestors will protect the new baby and bring the family luck. Red is a lucky color, so people often give gifts in red envelopes and eat red eggs. The baby often gets a hair cut on this special occasion.

1. Chinese families celebrate a baby's _____ or Moon Yuet.

2. They often eat _____ for luck.

3. Family members give presents in red _____.

4. In Chinese tradition, family _____ watch and protect the new baby.

5. _____ is a lucky color.

6. Parents often cut the baby's _____ on Moon Yuet.

D Answer the questions about your family traditions.

1. What is a tradition you and your family follow?

_____

2. What do you do?

_____

3. What do you wear or eat?

_____

FAMILY

LESSON

Use time outs.

A Read the letters. Complete the chart below.

Dear Dr. Dina,

I have two children, a son and a daughter. My son is 6 years old and my daughter is 4. Sometimes I have trouble handling their behavior. My son sometimes hits his sister when they are playng together. My daughter doesn't listen to me. For example, if I tell her to stop playing with her food, she still plays. I get so angry with them. What should I do?

Sincerely, Mad Mom

Dear Mad Mom,

It's hard to know how to discipline our children sometimes. You are a parent and your job is to keep children safe and help them learn. Children need to know how to follow rules. Here are some guidelines:

• **Use simple rules.**
• **Help your children use words. Teach your son how to tell his sister what he wants instead of hitting her.**
• **If you ignore small problems, they may go away. For example, compliment your daughter when she is eating properly, and ignore her when she plays with her food.**
• **Use time outs. Sometimes just taking your child away from the situation works.**
• **Reward good behavior.**
I hope these ideas help.

Dr. Dina

PROBLEMS (MAD MOM'S)	SOLUTIONS (DR. DINA'S IDEAS)

B Answer the questions.

1. How many children does the mother have? _____

2. What are the ages of the children? _____

3. What is the son's problem? _____

4. What is the daughter's problem? _____

5. Why is the mother writing? _____

6. What does Dr. Dina say a parent's job is? _____

_____

C Look at the picture. Answer the question below.

Is this a discipline problem? What would you do?

_____

_____

★ ★

TAKE IT OUTSIDE: Interview a family member, friend, or coworker. Write the answers.

1. What behavior problems do your children have? _____

_____

2. How do you discipline your children? _____

_____

★ ★

TAKE IT ONLINE: Search on the Internet using the words "disciplining children." Write down 2 ideas and share them with your classmates.

WORK
LESSON

Be a team player.

A Read the suggestions. Check *True, False,* or *I don't know* to the questions on page 103.

Getting Along With Others at Work

If you want to succeed in your job, you need to get along with your coworkers. Here are a few tips:

- Watch your coworkers and supervisor. See how they do things. Ask questions if you're not sure what to do.
- Don't take things personally. A coworker may say something that upsets you. Remember that he or she may just be in a bad mood.
- Tell people how you feel or ask questions in a clear and positive way. (For example: Thank you for showing me how to operate the machine. Could you show me how to use this, too?)
- Be a team player. Give ideas and suggestions to others.
- Compliment coworkers on their good work.
- Offer to help out when someone is sick.
- If someone criticizes you, ask how you can do a better job.

1. You shouldn't ask too many questions.   ☐ True   ☐ False   ☐ I don't know.
2. You should get upset at criticism.   ☐ True   ☐ False   ☐ I don't know.
3. You shouldn't give ideas to others.   ☐ True   ☐ False   ☐ I don't know.
4. You should compliment others.   ☐ True   ☐ False   ☐ I don't know.
5. You should be positive.   ☐ True   ☐ False   ☐ I don't know.

B Complete the sentences.

1. If someone upsets you at work, _____.

2. If you aren't sure what to do, _____.

3. If someone criticizes you, _____.

4. If a coworker does a good job, _____.

5. If a coworker is sick, _____.

C List 3 ideas you will try to get along with people better at work or school.

1. _____

2. _____

3. _____

★ ★

TAKE IT OUTSIDE: Interview a family member, friend, or coworker. Complete the survey.

AT WORK OR SCHOOL, HOW OFTEN DO YOU _____?	NEVER	SOMETIMES	ALWAYS
ask questions when you don't understand something			
get upset when someone says something negative			
compliment others on their good work			
ask for more information when you are criticized			
offer to help others			

★ ★

REVIEW

LESSON

Practice Test

DIRECTIONS: Choose the best answer. Use the Answer Sheet.

1. My son hit his sister. What should I do?

   A. Give him a time out.

   B. Take him to the doctor.

   C. Give him medicine.

   D. Give him money.

2. My supervisor criticized me. I should:

   A. get mad.

   B. call the police.

   C. ask how I can do better.

   D. get a new job.

3. Your dress looks very nice.

   A. I think it's terrible.

   B. Sorry.

   C. Thank you.

   D. You are very late.

4. You are very late.

   A. That's nice.

   B. I'm sorry.

   C. You are disorganized.

   D. Thank you.

5. My coworker complimented me today.

   A. That's nice.

   B. I'm sorry.

   C. You are disorganized.

   D. Thank you.

ANSWER SHEET				
1	A	B	C	D
2	A	B	C	D
3	A	B	C	D
4	A	B	C	D
5	A	B	C	D
6	A	B	C	D
7	A	B	C	D
8	A	B	C	D
9	A	B	C	D
10	A	B	C	D

6. My sister's son is my _____.

    A. uncle

    B. nephew

    C. niece

    D. aunt

7. Your mother is your daughter's _____.

    A. granddaughter

    B. grandparent

    C. mother

    D. aunt

8. The Martins live across the street. They are my _____.

    A. coworkers

    B. parents

    C. neighbors

    D. landlady

9. You have a problem with the sink in your apartment. You should call your _____.

    A. coworkers

    B. parents

    C. neighbors

    D. landlady

10. Ed's brother Tom got married today. Tom is the _____.

    A. fiancée

    B. bride

    C. uncle

    D. groom

HOW DID YOU DO? Count the number of correct answers on your answer sheet. Record this number in the bar graph on the inside back cover.

Spotlight: Grammar

TWO-WORD VERBS

- Some verbs have two words. The meaning of the two words together is different from the meaning of the separate words.

  EXAMPLES: Children **grow up.** (grow up = become adults)
                   The waiter **waited on** us right away. (waited on = took our food order)
                   She **called up** all her friends. (called up = telephoned)

- You can separate many two-word verbs with a noun or object pronoun.

  EXAMPLES: She **called** <u>her sister</u> **up.**
                   She **called** <u>her</u> **up.**

TIP
Object Pronouns
me   you
him   us
her   them
it

- A noun can go between or after the two words.   • An object pronoun can only go between the two words.

  EXAMPLES: He **looked up** <u>the word</u>.   Example: He **looked** <u>it</u> **up.**
                   He **looked** <u>the word</u> **up.**

A Write the words in the correct order. Then answer the questions. Use an object pronoun in place of the underlined noun.

1. (hand in / When / you / did / <u>the homework</u> / ?) *(give)*

   Question: *When did you hand in the homework*

   Answer: *I handed it in last Thursday*

2. (look up / Where / <u>a word</u> / did / you / ?)

   Question: *Where did you look up a word?*

   Answer: *I looked it up in the dictionary.*

3. (call up / <u>a friend</u> / last month / you / did / Why / ?)

   Question: *Why did you call up a friend last month?*

   Answer: *I called him up because I had question.*

4. (Why / turn down / <u>invitations</u> / should / you / ?)

   Question: *Why should you turn them down invitation?*

   Answer: *I should turn them down because I'm busy.*

5. (When / fill out / <u>registration forms</u> / do / you / ?)

   Question: *When do you fill out registration forms?*

   Answer: *I fill them out on the first day of school*

COUNT NOUNS AND NONCOUNT NOUNS

Count Nouns	Noncount Nouns

• Count nouns have a singular and a plural form.
  EXAMPLES: student—students
    brother—brothers
	• Noncount nouns are always singular.
	  EXAMPLES: money furniture
	    music coffee

• You can use *a* or *an* with the singular form of count nouns.
  EXAMPLES: a brother, an aunt, a family
	• You don't use *a* or *an* with noncount nouns.
	  EXAMPLES: I like music.
	    I love coffee.

• You can use *many, a lot of, a few,* and *any* with the plural form of count nouns.
  EXAMPLE: I have many aunts, a lot of cousins, and a few nieces. I don't have any nephews.
	• You can use *much, a lot of, a little,* and *any* with noncount nouns.
	  EXAMPLE: I drank too much coffee. I ate a lot of fruit and a little meat. I didn't eat any bread.

	• We often use quantity words with noncount nouns. EXAMPLE: I drank a cup of coffee. I bought a loaf of bread.

B Write the words in the correct place in the chart.

aunt	book	cereal	desk	friend	fruit	health
lettuce	money	photo	son	teacher	tree	water

COUNT NOUNS	NONCOUNT NOUNS
book aunt son desk tree friend lettce photo teacher	cereal fruit health money water

C Complete the sentences. Circle the correct answer.

1. I bought two ___breads___ .
   A. breads   B. loaves of bread

2. He has ___many___ sisters.
   A. many   B. much

3. They have ___a lot of___ money.
   A. a lot of   B. many

4. Do you need ___a___ stamp?
   A. any   B. a

5. Can she send ___three___ packages?
   A. too much   B. three

LESSON **1**

Muscles, Bones, and Joints

A Find these words in the puzzle. Circle them.

ankle	hip
arm	joint
back	knee
blood	leg
bone	lungs
brain	muscle
chest	shoulder
elbow	skin
ear	toe
finger	tooth
hand	waist
heart	wrist

```
m  u  s  c  l  e  g  o  t  o  e  f
b  a  c  k  u  h  i  p  o  q  u  i
r  j  o  i  n  t  b  l  o  o  d  n
a  r  m  z  g  d  o  j  t  p  a  g
i  h  w  v  s  t  n  r  h  o  n  e
n  s  k  i  n  h  e  a  r  t  k  r
b  c  i  w  a  i  s  t  f  e  l  h
e  l  b  o  w  r  i  s  t  a  e  a
x  l  s  h  o  u  l  d  e  r  i  n
c  h  e  s  t  k  n  e  e  v  p  d
```

B Complete the sentences with words from Activity A. You may need to make the words plural.

1. Ankles and shoulders are _____.

2. You use your _____ to move.

3. Your _____ covers and protects your body.

4. You use your _____ to eat your food.

5. You use your _____ to think.

6. A special muscle called the _____ pushes
   blood through your body.

7. Your _____ help you stand up.
   They give your body support, just like wood gives a building support.

8. You listen with your _____.

9. Pants often have a button at the _____.

10. If you lift something heavy, you can hurt your _____.

C Complete the sentences. Write *should* or *shouldn't*.

1. Jack hurt his knee. He _____ run.
2. Linda's tooth hurts. She _____ see a dentist.
3. If you want strong muscles, you _____ exercise often.
4. When your back hurts, you _____ rest.
5. If you want to be healthy, you _____ smoke cigarettes.
6. If they want to do well on the test, they _____ go to bed early.

should and *shouldn't*

D Look at the activities. Write them in the correct place in the chart.

exercise often   smoke cigarettes
get 8 hours of sleep   eat nutritious food
eat fatty food   see a doctor regularly
work too many hours   brush my teeth every day

IF I WANT TO BE HEALTHY,	
I should:	I shouldn't:

LESSON 2

Maybe you should see a doctor.

A Match the questions and answers.

Questions	Answers
1. _____ My skin is red. What's wrong with it?	a. I fell down the stairs.
2. _____ How do I know when I have the flu?	b. You might get a burn.
3. _____ What's a fracture?	c. Your joints ache, you have a fever, and you feel terrible.
4. _____ How did you get that bruise?	d. It looks like a rash.
5. _____ What will happen if you touch the hot stove?	e. It's a broken bone.

B Circle the correct answer.

1. I cut my finger and now it's red and smells bad. I think I have:

   A. an infection. B. a sprain.

2. Jorge fell and turned his ankle. He might have:

   A. the flu. B. a sprain.

3. My sister ate something bad. Now she is:

   A. bleeding. B. feeling nauseous.

4. My new shoes are too tight. They're giving me:

   A. a cold. B. a blister.

5. Don't touch that electric wire. You might get:

   A. a shock. B. a bruise.

C Answer the questions about you.

1. Did you have the flu last year? _____

2. Do you have a fever today? _____

3. Are you feeling dizzy now? _____

4. When do you feel nauseous? _____

5. How often do you get a cold? _____

D Look at the pictures. Write about the problems. Use *might* and *will*.

1. If you leave something on the floor, _____

_____

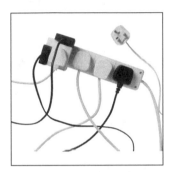

2. If you plug too many wires into one socket, _____

_____

3. If you turn around in a circle too fast, _____

_____

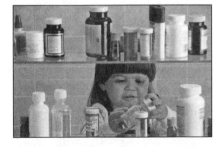

4. If a child takes medicine without permission, _____

_____

5. If you do dangerous sports, _____

_____

Did you go to the emergency room?

A Match the problems and the treatments.

Problems

1. I broke my arm.
2. I sprained my ankle.
3. I cut my hand.
4. I bruised my head.
5. I burned my finger.
6. I hurt my elbow.

Treatments

a. a cast
b. an ice pack
c. crutches
d. a sling
e. a bandage
f. stitches

B Write the words under the pictures.

| bandage | crutch | examining room | ice pack |
| splint | waiting room | wheelchair | x-ray |

1. _____

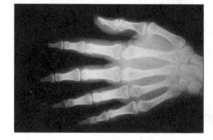

2. _____

3. _____

4. _____

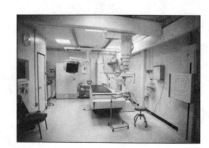

5. _____

C Put the conversation in order. Number the sentences from first (1) to last (6).

_____ Did you have to go to the emergency room?

_____ Yes, a friend took me.

_____ What happened to your elbow?

_____ Did they put ice on it?

_____ I sprained it.

_____ Yes, and then they gave me this sling.

D Answer the questions about you.

1. When did you have an injury? _____

2. What kind of injury was it? _____

3. What body part did you injure? _____

4. Did you go to the emergency room? _____

5. What did you do for the injury? _____

E Read the story. Underline the injury, the body part, and the treatment.

I sprained my ankle in 2002. I was running down a hill when I slipped. I went to the emergency room. They took x-rays, but they said I didn't have a fracture. The doctor put a bandage on my ankle and gave me some crutches.

F Write a story about your injury. Use your answers in Activity D. Follow the model in Activity E.

_____

_____

_____

_____

_____

_____

4
LESSON

Medicine Labels

A Write the words under the pictures.

tablet	teaspoon	cream	capsule

1. _____

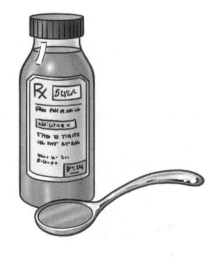

2. _____

3. _____

4. _____

B Complete the sentences.

1. 1 tbsp. = _____ tsp.

2. 12 tsp. = _____ tbsp.

3. 3 tbsp. = _____ fl. oz.

4. 2 fl. oz. = _____ tsp.

5. 9 tsp. = _____ fl. oz.

C Answer the questions.

1. You need to take 1/2 fluid ounce of a medicine. How many teaspoons is it? _____

2. Your child should take 1 1/2 teaspoons of medicine. How many tablespoons is it? _____

3. Your doctor told you to drink 4 fluid ounces of juice. How many tablespoons should you

   put in the glass? _____

D Read the label. Check *yes* or *no* to the questions below.

Marvelaid
225 Ibuprofen Tablets, 200 mg.

Active ingredient (in each tablet):
Ibuprofen 200 mg
Uses: Reduces fever and relieves
aches and pains due to:
• headache
• muscular aches
• backache
• the common cold
• toothache
Directions:
• Do not take more than directed.
• Adults: take 1 tablet every 4 to 6
  hours while symptoms occur.
• If pain or fever is not reduced, you
  may take 2 tablets.
• The smallest effective dose should
  be used.
• Children: do not give to children
  under 12.

1. This medicine is for fever and pain. ☐ yes ☐ no

2. There are 200 tablets in the container. ☐ yes ☐ no

3. Adults and children should take Marvelaid. ☐ yes ☐ no

4. This can help if you have a toothache. ☐ yes ☐ no

5. You can take one tablet every two hours. ☐ yes ☐ no

E Write 2 warnings, or things you shouldn't do with this medicine.

1. You shouldn't _____.

2. You shouldn't _____.

FAMILY

LESSON

What is her father's health problem?

A Read the medical history form. Answer the questions below.

Medical History Form

Name: Last	First	MI	Birthdate	Sex
Park	Grace	S.	5/19/72	Female

Address	City	State	Zip
6517 South Elm St.	Bradford	MI	49503

Person to notify in case of emergency	Relationship	Telephone number
Elizabeth Park	sister	555-8043

	Age	Occupation	Significant medical problems
Father	62	store owner	heart disease
Mother	59	accountant	none
Sister	27	dentist	bad headaches
Brother	37	librarian	none

Have you had any of the following? Check *yes* or *no*. Explain if you answer *yes*.

Heart problems _____	☐ yes	☐ no
Lung problems _____	☐ yes	☐ no
Bleeding problems _____	☐ yes	☐ no
Bad headaches _____	☐ yes	☐ no
Repeated infections _____	☐ yes	☐ no
Repeated earaches __I get earaches several times a year.__	☑ yes	☐ no
Allergies _____	☐ yes	☐ no

---

1. What is the patient's name? _____

2. What is her father's health problem? _____

3. Does her mother have a health problem? _____

4. Who should someone call if there is an emergency? _____

5. What problem does the patient sometimes have? _____

B Complete the medical history form for you.

Medical History Form

Name: Last	First	MI	Birthdate	Sex
Address	City	State	Zip	

Person to notify in case of emergency	Relationship	Telephone number

	Age	Occupation	Significant medical problems
Father			
Mother			
Sister			
Brother			

Have you had any of the following? Check *yes* or *no*. Explain if you answer *yes*.

Heart problems _____ ☐ yes ☐ no

Lung problems _____ ☐ yes ☐ no

Bleeding problems _____ ☐ yes ☐ no

Bad headaches _____ ☐ yes ☐ no

Repeated infections _____ ☐ yes ☐ no

Repeated earaches _____ ☐ yes ☐ no

Allergies _____ ☐ yes ☐ no

★ ★

TAKE IT OUTSIDE: Interview a family member, friend, or coworker. Write the answers.

1. What kind of health problems do you have?

   _____

2. Did you have any serious injuries when you were a child? If yes, what were they?

   _____

3. Does anyone in your family have serious health problems?

   _____

★ ★

COMMUNITY
LESSON

When should you go to the ER?

A Read about health care services. Circle the words that are new to you.

convulsion	numbness	urgent	vomiting

When should you go to an emergency room?

Go to the emergency room when you have a serious medical condition or symptom (including severe pain) caused by an injury or illness, which happens suddenly. The ER is for situations where you may die if you don't get treatment right away.

Some examples include:

- Signs of a heart attack that last two minutes or longer, including chest pain
- Signs of stroke, like sudden onset of numbness in arms or legs
- Severe shortness of breath
- Bleeding that won't stop
- Poisoning
- Bad fractures
- Major injury such as head injury
- Coughing up or vomiting blood

When can you go to an urgent care center?

"Urgent care" is care that can wait for the time it takes to call your doctor for instructions on treatment. Your doctor can tell you if you should go to an urgent care center or come to the office.

Examples of problems your doctor or an urgent care center can treat:

- Earaches
- Minor cuts where bleeding is controlled
- Sprains
- Skin rashes
- Colds, coughs, sore throat
- Most fevers, though if there is a convulsion or extreme fever in a child, go to the ER

If you have any questions about whether it is an emergency or not, you should call your primary care physician.

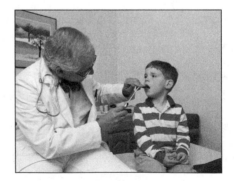

B Write the definitions.

The emergency room: _____

An urgent care center: _____

C Check *the emergency room* or *an urgent care center*.

IF YOU HAVE THIS PROBLEM, YOU SHOULD GO TO:	THE EMERGENCY ROOM	AN URGENT CARE CENTER
a heart attack		
an earache		
severe bleeding that won't stop		
a bad cold		
a bad fracture		

D Answer the questions.

1. If you have the flu, should you go to the emergency room or call your doctor?

   _____

2. If you cut your hand and you can't stop the bleeding, where should you go?

   _____

3. What might happen if you have a heart attack and you don't go to the emergency room?

   _____

4. Which do you think you should use more often, the emergency room or an urgent care center?

   _____

★ ★

TAKE IT OUTSIDE: Interview a family member, friend, or coworker. Write the answers.

1. Do you ever go to the emergency room at the hospital? Why or why not?

   _____

   _____

★ ★

TAKE IT ONLINE: Search the Internet for the names of 2 hospitals with emergency rooms and 2 urgent care centers in your area. Write the names and addresses. Keep the information where you can find it quickly in an emergency.

Practice Test

DIRECTIONS: Look at the sign to answer the next 5 questions. Use the Answer Sheet.

Urgent Care Center

Monday–Thursday 8:00 A.M. – 7:00 P.M.

Friday–Sunday 9:00 A.M. – 9:00 P.M.

---

1. You sprained your ankle on Monday at 7:30 P.M. When can you go to the Urgent Care Center?
   A. At 8:00 A.M. on Tuesday.
   B. At 7:30 P.M. on Monday.
   C. Yes, you can.
   D. No, you can't.

2. You have a bad cold. It is 9:00 A.M. on Sunday. When can you go to the Urgent Care Center?
   A. Yes, it is.
   B. No, it isn't.
   C. At 9:00 A.M. on Sunday.
   D. At 8:00 A.M. on Monday.

3. You have an infection. You work from 7:00 A.M. until 7:00 P.M. Monday through Friday. When can you go to the Urgent Care Center?
   A. Monday – Thursday
   B. every day
   C. Friday – Sunday
   D. Monday – Friday

4. What time does the center open on Saturday?
   A. 8:00 A.M.
   B. 9:00 A.M.
   C. 7:00 P.M.
   D. 9:00 P.M.

5. You are having a heart attack on Tuesday night. Where should you go?
   A. Yes, you should.
   B. No, you shouldn't.
   C. To the emergency room.
   D. To the urgent care center.

ANSWER SHEET

1. Ⓐ Ⓑ Ⓒ Ⓓ
2. Ⓐ Ⓑ Ⓒ Ⓓ
3. Ⓐ Ⓑ Ⓒ Ⓓ
4. Ⓐ Ⓑ Ⓒ Ⓓ
5. Ⓐ Ⓑ Ⓒ Ⓓ
6. Ⓐ Ⓑ Ⓒ Ⓓ
7. Ⓐ Ⓑ Ⓒ Ⓓ
8. Ⓐ Ⓑ Ⓒ Ⓓ
9. Ⓐ Ⓑ Ⓒ Ⓓ
10. Ⓐ Ⓑ Ⓒ Ⓓ

DIRECTIONS: Look at the accident report to answer the next 5 questions. Use the Answer Sheet on page 120.

ACCIDENT REPORT

Name of person injured: _____ ① _____

Address: _____ ② _____

How did the accident happen? _____ ③ _____

_____

Part of the Body Injured		Type of Injury
☐ ankle ☐ foot		☐ bruise
☐ arm ☐ hand ④		☐ burn ⑤
☐ back ☐ head		☐ cut
☐ chest ☐ knee		☐ fracture
☐ elbow ☐ leg		☐ sprain
☐ finger ☐ shoulder		

Supervisor's signature _____ ⑥ _____ Date _____ ⑦ _____

6. Sam cut his hand. Where would you write it was a "cut"?
   A. Part 3
   B. Part 4
   C. Part 5
   D. Part 6

7. Ricardo Lopez had an accident. Where would you write his name?
   A. Part 1
   B. Part 2
   C. Part 3
   D. Part 4

8. The supervisor has to fill out the accident report. Where would she sign her name?
   A. Part 4
   B. Part 5
   C. Part 6
   D. Part 7

9. Where would you write that an employee hurt her finger?
   A. Part 4
   B. Part 5
   C. Part 6
   D. Part 7

10. Where would you explain how someone got hurt?
   A. Part 1
   B. Part 2
   C. Part 3
   D. Part 4

HOW DID YOU DO? Count the number of correct answers on your answer sheet. Record this number in the bar graph on the inside back cover.

121

LESSON 1

Did I unplug the coffeepot?

A Look at the picture. Write 1 or more objects next to each action.

door	eggs	heat	juice cup
pan	pot	refrigerator	stove

1. take out   *a pot* _____
2. turn down _____
3. unplug _____
4. lock _____
5. shut off _____
6. put back _____

B Write a story about the picture. Use words from Activity A. Write 4 sentences.

EXAMPLE: The man is the baby's father. He is making breakfast.

_____
_____
_____
_____

C Answer the questions about you.

1. What did you shut off today? _____

2. What did you turn on yesterday? _____

3. What do you usually turn off at night? _____

4. What do you lock? _____

5. What do you unplug when you go away? _____

D Rewrite the polite requests as commands.

1. Would you please unplug the computer?

   _____

2. Could you turn off your cell phone, please?

   _____

3. Would you please lock the door?

   _____

4. Could you please turn down the radio?

   _____

5. Would you take out your books, please?

   _____

E Write a polite request to solve each problem.

1. Your neighbor is playing very loud music.

   _____

2. Your coworker accidentally unplugged the copier.

   _____

The sink's leaking.

A Write a sentence about each picture. Tell about a problem. Use the words in parentheses.

1. _____

_____ (leak)

2. _____

_____ (overheat)

3. _____

_____ (plugged up)

B Answer the questions.

1. What problems did you have in your home last year? _____

2. Who can fix a leaking toilet for you? _____

3. Who do you call when an elevator is stuck? _____

C Put the conversation in order. Number the sentences from first (1) to last (6).

_____ Could you please take a look at my shower again?

_____ No. This time it's plugged up.

_____ Hello. This is Mike Burnett in apartment 2H.

_____ Is it leaking again?

_____ Okay. I'll be over as soon as I can.

_____ Hi. What can I do for you?

D Complete the sentences. Write *will* or *won't*.

1. I have an appointment tomorrow so I _____ be in class.

2. She _____ call when the car is ready. Then we can pick it up.

3. If the roof leaks again, he _____ call a roofing company.

4. I _____ take a bath if the bathtub is plugged up.

5. If the space heater is too close to the curtains, it _____ start a fire.

will/won't

E Read about the problem. Complete the maintenance request form.

Carrie Wesley's toilet is leaking. It is 10:00 A.M. on the 12th of March, 2006. She lives in Apartment 10J at 201 Appleton Lane.

MAINTENANCE REQUEST FORM	
Date	
Time	
Name	
Address	
Problem	

Fire!

A Look at the picture. Check what you see.

- ❏ ambulance
- ❏ fire escape
- ❏ firefighter
- ❏ fire truck
- ❏ hose
- ❏ hydrant
- ❏ ladder
- ❏ smoke

B Complete the sentences.

ACROSS

1. When you are very sick or injured, an _____ can take you to the hospital.

3. A fire _____ has hoses and ladders on it.

6. You can climb up to the roof with a _____.

7. You can put water on your garden with a _____.

8. Firefighters _____ water on the fire.

DOWN

1. Please _____ a photo to your application.

2. If there is a fire in your home, you should _____ on the floor. The air is clearer there.

4. If you don't want too much sun, you can _____ your head with a hat.

5. Firefighters have to open up a _____ to get water.

8. It's very hard to breathe when there is a lot of _____.

C Write the words in the crossword puzzle.

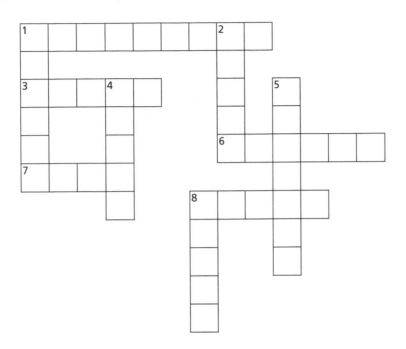

D Look at the graph. Circle the correct answer below.

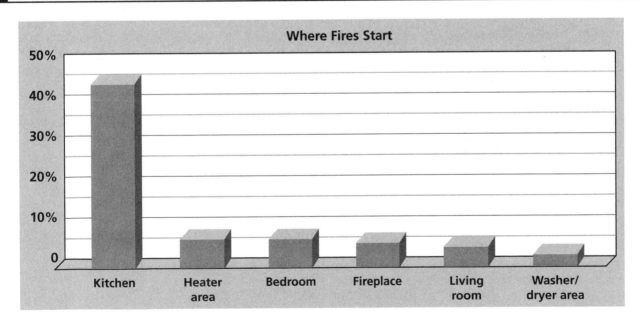

1. Where do most fires start in the house?

   A. in the living room   B. in the kitchen

2. Do more fires start near the heater or near the dryer?

   A. near the heater   B. near the dryer

3. What percentage of fires start in the bedroom?

   A. 7%   B. 3%

4. What percentage of fires start in the kitchen?

   A. 45%   B. 4.5%

An Emergency Situation

LESSON 4

A Look at the picture and the title of the reading. Check the emergency.

❏ flood   ❏ earthquake

❏ hurricane   ❏ tornado

EARTHQUAKE PROCEDURES

An earthquake will usually occur without any type of warning. DO NOT GO OUTSIDE THE BUILDING. Movement of the ground is <u>seldom</u> the actual cause of death or injury. Most injuries result from <u>partial</u> building collapse and falling objects, like <u>toppling</u> chimneys, ceiling plaster, and light fixtures.

During the shaking:

- **IF INDOORS, STAY THERE.** Protect yourself by taking cover under a table, desk, or supported doorway, or crouch against an interior wall. Do not stand under light fixtures, near bookcases, etc. If possible, plan a safe location to take cover in an earthquake.
- Do not leave cover until instructed to do so.
- Do not use elevators.
- **IF OUTDOORS** get into an open area away from trees, buildings, walls, and power lines.

After the shaking:

- Check for injuries.
- Check for fire. Turn off gas.

B Read the information on earthquake procedures. Circle *should* or *shouldn't*.

EXAMPLE: You (should / shouldn't) go outside during an earthquake.

1. You (should / shouldn't) stand near a bookcase.

2. You (should / shouldn't) go under a table.

3. You (should / shouldn't) use elevators.

4. You (should / shouldn't) go under a tree if you are outside.

5. You (should / shouldn't) turn on the gas.

C Look at the underlined words in the reading. Match the words and the definitions.

Words
1. partial
2. seldom
3. toppling

Definitions
a. not very often
b. not whole, just part
c. falling

D Circle the correct answer.

1. How can you get hurt in an earthquake?
   A. movement of the ground   B. falling objects

2. Where should you go if you are outside?
   A. under a tree   B. to a open space

3. What should you do if you are inside?
   A. crawl under a desk   B. stand under a light

4. How can you tell if there is going to be an earthquake?
   A. You can't.   B. Pay attention to the warnings.

5. What should you check for after an earthquake?
   A. injuries   B. your wallet

E Convert the temperatures.

1. 100° C = _____° F

2. 0° C = _____° F

3. 59° F = _____° C

4. 77° F = _____° C

COMMUNITY

LESSON

Listen to the radio broadcast.

A Match each picture to a section of the reading on page 131. Write the numbers next to the pictures.

A.

_____

B.

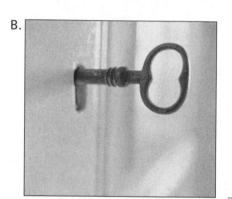

_____

C.

_____

E.

_____

D.

_____

B Read the information. Circle the words that are new to you.

authorized	broadcast	evacuate/evacuation	government	threat

Community Evacuation Plan

Local government will order an evacuation if there is a threat to the community and there is time to evacuate safely.

1. **Radio and Television:** Broadcasts will tell you when you have to evacuate.

2. **Children:** If you have children in school, go to the pick-up center named by the school.

3. **House:** Lock your house.

4. **Transportation:** Use your own car if you can. Take neighbors who need a ride, if you have room. If you don't have a car, ask one of your neighbors for a ride. If you cannot do that, go to one of the pick-up points along a main road. You can get a ride there.

5. **When you're leaving:** Keep all car windows and vents closed and drive (or walk) to the nearest main route in your area. Turn on your car radio for information. Police and other authorized personnel will be along main roads to direct you.

C Complete the sentences with words from the reading.

1. _____ will order an evacuation.

2. When you _____, you leave your home and go to a safe place.

3. You will get information on the evacuation from radio and television _____.

4. A _____ is something that can hurt you.

5. _____ personnel are people who can tell you what to do in an emergency.

★ ★

TAKE IT OUTSIDE: Interview a friend, family member, or coworker. Write the answers.

Do you have a family emergency plan?	Where would you go in an evacuation?	What do you think you need in an evacuation?

★ ★

 TAKE IT ONLINE: Use the Internet to search for "evacuation plan." Write down 3 things you should do if there is an evacuation in your town or city.

WORK

LESSON

Go to the nearest safe exit.

A Look at the safety equipment. Write the words under the pictures.

| fire extinguisher | fire alarm | smoke detector |

1. _____   2. _____   3. _____

B Match the equipment and the purposes.

Equipment

1. _____ fire alarm

2. _____ fire extinguisher

3. _____ smoke detector

Purposes

a. It makes a noise when there is smoke.

b. If you pull this, it makes a noise to tell people there is a fire.

c. You can spray this on a fire to put it out.

C Read the procedures. Check *True* or *False* to the questions on page 133.

AT THE SOUND OF A FIRE ALARM:

1. Go to the nearest safe exit and go outside.

2. WALK. Do not run. Shut all doors behind you and proceed along corridors in a quiet, orderly manner. Do not push.

3. Proceed to the assembly area for your building. Keep back a minimum of 300 feet from the building.

4. **DO NOT GO BACK INTO THE BUILDING FOR ANY REASON UNTIL THE FIRE DEPARTMENT HAS GIVEN ITS PERMISSION TO DO SO.**

If there is a fire,

1. you should run outside.   ❑ True   ❑ False
2. you should shut doors behind you.   ❑ True   ❑ False
3. you shouldn't push.   ❑ True   ❑ False
4. you should stay behind to help others.   ❑ True   ❑ False
5. you should go 100 feet from the building.   ❑ True   ❑ False

D   Answer the questions.

1. Is there a fire extinguisher at your work or school?

   _____

2. Where is the closest fire exit at school?

   _____

3. If there is a fire at your work or school, where are you supposed to go?

   _____

★ ★

TAKE IT OUTSIDE: Interview a family member, friend, or coworker. Complete the chart.

WHERE DO YOU WORK?	WHAT SAFETY EQUIPMENT DO YOU HAVE AT WORK?	WHAT DO YOU DO IF THERE IS A FIRE AT WORK?

★ ★

 TAKE IT ONLINE: Use the Internet to search for "smoke detectors" or "smoke alarms" + your town or city. Write down 2 places where you can buy one.

Practice Test

DIRECTIONS: Look at the form to answer the next 5 questions. Use the Answer Sheet.

MAINTENANCE REQUEST FORM		
Date	5/19/05	**Line 1**
Time	8:45 P.M.	**Line 2**
Name	Nadia Thomas	**Line 3**
Address	1201 Willow Street	**Line 4**
Problem	sliding glass door stuck	**Line 5**

1. On what line should you write your name?

   A. Line 1

   B. Line 2

   C. Line 3

   D. Line 4

2. Your toilet is leaking. Where do you write this?

   A. Line 2

   B. Line 3

   C. Line 4

   D. Line 5

3. You live in Apartment 13A. Where should you write this?

   A. Line 1

   B. Line 2

   C. Line 3

   D. Line 4

4. What is Nadia's problem?

   A. Her toilet is leaking.

   B. Her sliding door is stuck.

   C. Her oven is overheating.

   D. Her front door is stuck.

5. What time is it?

   A. 5:19

   B. 5:05

   C. 8:45

   D. 12:01

ANSWER SHEET

1	Ⓐ	Ⓑ	Ⓒ	Ⓓ
2	Ⓐ	Ⓑ	Ⓒ	Ⓓ
3	Ⓐ	Ⓑ	Ⓒ	Ⓓ
4	Ⓐ	Ⓑ	Ⓒ	Ⓓ
5	Ⓐ	Ⓑ	Ⓒ	Ⓓ
6	Ⓐ	Ⓑ	Ⓒ	Ⓓ
7	Ⓐ	Ⓑ	Ⓒ	Ⓓ
8	Ⓐ	Ⓑ	Ⓒ	Ⓓ
9	Ⓐ	Ⓑ	Ⓒ	Ⓓ
10	Ⓐ	Ⓑ	Ⓒ	Ⓓ

DIRECTIONS: Look at the emergency procedures to answer the next 5 questions. Use the Answer Sheet on page 134.

TORNADO

In the event of a tornado:

1. Stay inside and listen to the radio.
2. Close doors and shut off equipment.
3. Move everyone to a safe area within the building.
4. Ensure that everyone is under sturdy furniture and using their arms to protect their heads.
5. After the tornado passes, check for injuries.

---

6. What should you shut off?

   A. the radio

   B. equipment

   C. doors

   D. furniture

7. What should you listen to?

   A. the radio

   B. equipment

   C. doors

   D. furniture

8. What should you close?

   A. the radio

   B. equipment

   C. doors

   D. furniture

9. Where should you go?

   A. outside

   B. under a tree

   C. under a desk

   D. to the exit

10. Where can you get information during a tornado?

   A. from the radio

   B. from the police

   C. on television

   D. over the telephone

HOW DID YOU DO? Count the number of correct answers on your answer sheet. Record this number in the bar graph on the inside back cover.

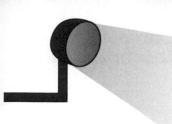

Spotlight: Grammar

FUTURE WITH *WILL*		
Statements	**Contractions**	
	Affirmative	*Negative*
I	I'll	I won't
He	he'll	he won't
She **will** be there tomorrow.	she'll	she won't
It **won't** be here tomorrow.	it'll	it won't
You	you'll	you won't
We **won't = will not**	we'll	we won't
They	they'll	they won't

A   Complete the sentences. Write *will* or *won't.*

1. I have to work tomorrow night. I _____ be able to come to your party.

2. I know Juan's coming. He _____ be here soon.

3. Their friends are coming this weekend. They _____ have to get some more food.

4. She has to go to New York. She _____ be in class for a few days.

5. We have a lot to do today. We _____ have any free time.

6. Nadia has a test tomorrow. I'm sure she _____ be in class. She wants to do well.

7. What can you bring to the party? Tom _____ bring soda, so we don't need that.

8. There's a storm coming. We _____ watch the news to find out about class tomorrow.

B   Write short answers. Use *will* or *won't.*

1. Will you go to another country next year?

_____

2. Will your parents come to visit soon?

_____

3. Will you get married this year?

_____

FUTURE CONDITIONAL STATEMENTS

- Conditional statements with *will* and *won't:*
  If it rains tomorrow, we **won't have** a picnic.
  If I stay up late tonight, **I'll feel** tired tomorrow.
- Conditional statements with *might* and *might not:*
  If you eat too much, you **might get** sick.
  If you don't study, you **might not pass** the test.
- Conditional statements with *should* and *shouldn't:*
  If it gets cold tonight, you **should turn up** the heat.
  If you feel sick tomorrow, you **shouldn't go** to work.

TIP

- Future conditional statements tell what will or might happen in the future under certain conditions.

       (condition)   *(result)*
  If she studies hard this week, she will pass the test.

- Use the simple present in the *if* clause.
  If I <u>feel</u> tired tomorrow, I might stay home.

- Use *will* to describe a definite future result. Use *might* to describe a possible future result. Use *should* to give advice.

C Answer the questions.

1. What will you do if you win a lot of money?

   _____

2. What will happen if there is a tornado during class tomorrow?

   _____

3. If there is a fire at your house, what should you do?

   _____

4. If you don't study, what might happen?

   _____

5. If you want to get a new job, what should you do?

   _____

6. If there is an earthquake, what will you do?

   _____

LESSON

She works with numbers.

A Write the words under the pictures.

| administration | health care | construction | manufacturing |

A.

1. _____
2. _____

B.

1. _____
2. _____

C.

1. _____
2. _____

D.

1. _____
2. _____

B Write 2 jobs under each workplace in Activity A.

C Match the jobs and the skills.

Jobs	Skills
1. a dental assistant	a. cleans teeth
2. a computer programmer	b. puts bricks together
3. a welder	c. uses a computer
4. a bricklayer	d. works with metal
5. a machine operator	e. takes care of sick people
6. a nursing assistant	f. runs machines in a factory

D Complete the sentences. Write *has to, have to, doesn't have to*, or *don't have to*.

1. A student _____ go to class.

2. Parents _____ take care of their children.

3. Children _____ work.

4. A teacher _____ bring food to class.

5. Students _____ study to do well in class.

6. We _____ eat.

7. We _____ make a million dollars.

8. A dental assistant _____ wash his hands.

9. A machine operator _____ have a college degree.

10. Bricklayers _____ wear ties to work.

E Answer the questions about you.

1. Do you have to work? _____

2. What do you have to do every day? _____

3. Do you have to do homework? _____

4. Do you have to fix your car? _____

5. What do you think a teacher has to do? _____

F Write 3 sentences about what you have to do if you want to be a good student.

_____

_____

_____

139

LESSON 2

He works well with others.

A Look at the picture. List 4 job skills she needs.

1. _____

2. _____

3. _____

4. _____

B Circle the correct answer.

1. Can he follow directions well?
   A. I think so.   B. No, he didn't.

2. Is she punctual?
   A. Yes, she does.   B. No, she isn't.

3. Are they dependable?
   A. Yes, they can.   B. No, they aren't.

4. Do you work well with others?
   A. Yes, I do.   B. No, I am not.

5. Does the job require computer skills?
   A. Yes, it does.   B. No, you don't.

C Answer the questions about you. Use *can, can't, do, don't, am, am not, did,* or *didn't.*

1. Do you work well with others? _____

2. Can you work independently? _____

3. Are you good at following directions? _____

4. Are you always punctual? _____

5. Did you solve problems in your last job? _____

6. Do you have excellent computer skills? _____

7. Can you fix electrical problems? _____

D Compare the skills a welder and an accountant need. Write 2 skills in each category.

Skills a welder needs   Skills both jobs need   Skills an accountant needs

E Complete the sentences. Write *would like* or *wouldn't like.*

1. My sister loves to take care of people. She _____ to be a nursing assistant.

2. Ali dislikes computers. He _____ to be a computer programmer.

3. They are learning how to fix electrical problems. They _____ to be electricians.

4. A coworker is a dental assistant now. She wants to go back to school because she _____ to be a dentist.

5. I don't like to talk to people. I _____ a job answering phones.

F Answer the questions about you.

1. Would you rather work with others or work independently?

_____

2. Would you rather be a dental assistant or a bricklayer?

_____

LESSON 3

I'd rather work full time.

A Find these words in the puzzle. Circle them.

assembler	office
caregiver	painter
computer	problem
cubicle	punctual
electrician	shift
machine	supply
night	welder

```
a  c  o  m  p  u  t  e  r  i  z  e  k
p  u  n  c  t  u  a  l  e  n  d  s  c
a  b  s  g  c  a  r  e  g  i  v  e  r
s  i  u  o  f  f  i  c  e  x  i  t  e
s  c  p  s  h  i  f  t  u  p  o  t  a
e  l  p  i  o  c  p  r  o  b  l  e  m
m  e  l  n  e  p  a  i  n  t  e  r  s
b  a  y  g  y  z  i  c  v  u  t  h  e
l  r  n  m  a  c  h  i  n  e  s  v  t
e  w  e  l  d  e  r  a  b  l  e  n  d
r  u  l  i  k  e  a  n  i  g  h  t  x
```

B Match the questions and answers.

Questions	Answers
1. ____ Do you have any experience as a painter?	a. I'd rather work full time.
2. ____ Are you good at working independently?	b. Yes, I do. I worked as a painter in my country.
3. ____ Would you rather work full time or part time?	c. Yes, I am. I had to work independently in my last job.
4. ____ Would you rather work days or evenings?	d. I like both.
5. ____ Would you prefer to work inside or outside?	e. I prefer days, but I can do either.

C Answer the questions about you.

1. Would you rather work full time or part time?

_____

2. Do you prefer days or evenings?

_____

3. Would you like to work inside or outside?

_____

4. Would you rather go to school full time or work full time?

_____

D Read the story. Check *True* or *False* below.

Gil works too hard. He is working full time as an accountant during the day. He also works part time in the evenings as a salesclerk at the department store. Gil is saving money. He is going to get married and wants to buy a house. He would rather work days only. After he gets married, Gil is going to quit his job at the department store.

1. Gil works full time at a department store.
   ☐ True   ☐ False
2. He is going to get married.
   ☐ True   ☐ False
3. He prefers to work in the evenings.
   ☐ True   ☐ False
4. He wants to buy a house.
   ☐ True   ☐ False
5. He is going to quit one of his jobs.
   ☐ True   ☐ False

143

4 **LESSON**

Starting a New Job

A Read the information on the website. Check the suggestions that are on the website.

Starting a New Job

Starting a New Job

Start off on the right foot
So you're starting a new job soon. Congratulations! Of course you're a little nervous. You can begin right now to make a good start. You need to organize:

- What to wear
- Your transportation
- Childcare, if necessary

What to wear
You need to wear clothes that meet the dress code at work. In some workplaces, you will wear a uniform, in others, you need business attire, and in some you'll wear casual or dress casual clothes.

Uniforms: If your new employer did not tell you where to get your uniform, look up "uniforms" in the telephone book. Call and ask if the store has what you need.

Business/casual attire: Business attire usually means a suit, or a coat and tie for men, and a suit or jacket and dress for women. Of course you can go to a department store for business or casual attire. Thrift shops also carry business clothes at a cheaper price.

Transportation

Transportation

- How will you get to work? Make a plan now. Do a practice trip so you know how long it will take.
- Plan for extra time. Make sure you add 15–30 minutes in case there is a problem.
- Have a back-up plan. What if something does go wrong (the car won't start)? You need to have another way to get there.
- Call if you are going to be late.

Childcare

Childcare

- Get childcare now. Contact your local Child Care Resource Agency.
- Ask other parents for referrals.
- Get medical forms completed and any necessary immunizations.
- Have emergency contact information available.

Suggestions:

- ☐ Be on time.
- ☐ Go to a thrift store for better prices.
- ☐ Call if you are going to be late.
- ☐ Have a back-up plan.
- ☐ Get a bus schedule.

- ☐ Talk to other parents.
- ☐ Fill out medical forms.
- ☐ Look in the telephone book for "uniforms."
- ☐ Plan for extra time.

B Write the suggestions from Activity A in the correct place in the chart.

WHAT TO WEAR	CHILDCARE	TRANSPORTATION

C Write a solution from the reading for each problem.

PROBLEM	SOLUTION
You don't have much money for clothes.	
Your car won't start the first day.	
Your child has an emergency at childcare and you aren't available.	
You need a uniform.	
You're not sure how long it takes to get to your new job.	

D Evaluate the information on the website. List 3 ideas that were the most useful for you.

1. _____

2. _____

3. _____

FAMILY

LESSON

What is most important to you?

A Look at the picture. Write 3 sentences about what you see.

1. _____

2. _____

3. _____

B Read the information about 2 childcare centers. Complete the sentences on page 147.

INFORMATION	KID'S WORLD LEARNING CENTER	WEE CARE LEARNING CENTER
License number	60000971	6055065
Approved to transport children	Yes	Yes
Date of inspection	10/15/03	3/12/03
Classification	Superior	Superior
Score (out of 235 points)	222	227
Cost per week	$165	$131
Meals provided	Breakfast, lunch, snacks	Snacks, lunch
Hours for full time care	6–10 per day	4–12 per day
Ratio of teachers to children	1:15	1:20
Discount for second child	10%	5%

1. The names of the two centers are _____ and _____.

2. Kid's World costs _____ per week.

3. Wee Care costs _____ per week.

4. At Wee Care, they can have _____ children for each teacher.

5. If you want to have two children in childcare at Kid's World, the discount for the second child is _____%.

C Write the advantages of each center in the chart below. In what ways is one better than the other?

KID'S WORLD	WEE CARE
serves breakfast	costs less per week

★ ★

TAKE IT OUTSIDE: Interview a family member, friend, or coworker who is also a parent. Write the answers.

Name of person interviewed: _____

1. What is most important to you in finding childcare—cost, location, schedule, or the number of children in the class? Why? _____

_____

_____

_____.

★ ★

TAKE IT ONLINE: Use the Internet to search for "childcare" + the name of your city or town. Write the names and numbers of 3 childcare centers.

She wears business casual clothes.

A Look at the picture. Check the type of work clothes you see.

❏ Business attire

❏ Casual

❏ Uniform

B Read the story. Circle the correct answers to the questions below.

Monica Jen got a new job two years ago. She started working for a company that designs and builds new office buildings. Monica was still a student and didn't have much money. She didn't have to wear business attire except to important meetings, but she did need to wear "business casual" clothes. That meant no jeans or T-shirts.

Monica looked up "thrift shops" in the yellow pages of the telephone book. She went to three of the stores and found some very nice used clothing. She bought several outfits for less than $50.

Now Monica has a lot more money for clothes. Some of her clothes are still good but they don't fit anymore. Monica found out about an organization called Dress for Success. This organization gives suits to people who don't have money so they can go to job interviews. Monica gave her suits to Dress for Success.

1. What happened two years ago?
   A. Monica started school.
   B. Monica started a new job.

2. What kind of clothes did Monica have to get for work?
   A. suits and business casual clothes
   B. T-shirts and jeans

3. Why did she decide to go to thrift shops for clothes?

    A. She didn't have a lot of money.   B. They have new clothes.

4. How did she find information on thrift shops?

    A. She asked Dress for Success.   B. She looked in the yellow pages.

5. Where did she donate her old suits?

    A. Dress for Success   B. a thrift shop

C Answer the questions about you.

1. What kind of clothes do you wear most often?

    _____

2. How much money do you spend on your clothes each year? _____

3. Where do you buy your clothes? _____

4. What do you think is the best way to save money on clothes?

    _____

5. What do you do with old clothes or household items?

    _____

★ ★

TAKE IT OUTSIDE: Interview 3 people. Write their answers.

NAME	WHAT DO YOU DO WITH OLD CLOTHES OR HOUSEHOLD ITEMS?

★ ★

TAKE IT ONLINE: Use the Internet to search for "donate clothing" + the name of your city or town. Write down 3 places where you can donate your clothes.

149

LESSON

Practice Test

DIRECTIONS: Look at the ads to answer the next 5 questions. Use the Answer Sheet.

---

1 ADMINISTRATIVE ASST.
Strong customer service skills. Some computer work. Moorseville area. Fax resume: 828-555-9000 or mail to P.O. Box 1380, Moorseville, UT

2 NURSING ASSISTANTS
CNA'S needed for nursing home in Marsh Hill. No experience necessary. Call (451)555-9878.

3 CONSTRUCTION/PAINTING
Wanted: Pinehurst area company seeking person with painting and carpentry experience. Must have references, valid driver's license, and good driving history. Call (303)555-1256.

4 ACCOUNTS PAYABLE CLERK
Fast growing home builder needs accounts payable clerk. Computer skills necessary. Must have good knowledge of accounting. Construction experience preferred. Please fax resume to (414)555-1232.

ANSWER SHEET

	A	B	C	D
1	Ⓐ	Ⓑ	Ⓒ	Ⓓ
2	Ⓐ	Ⓑ	Ⓒ	Ⓓ
3	Ⓐ	Ⓑ	Ⓒ	Ⓓ
4	Ⓐ	Ⓑ	Ⓒ	Ⓓ
5	Ⓐ	Ⓑ	Ⓒ	Ⓓ
6	Ⓐ	Ⓑ	Ⓒ	Ⓓ
7	Ⓐ	Ⓑ	Ⓒ	Ⓓ
8	Ⓐ	Ⓑ	Ⓒ	Ⓓ
9	Ⓐ	Ⓑ	Ⓒ	Ⓓ
10	Ⓐ	Ⓑ	Ⓒ	Ⓓ

---

1. You want to apply for the administrative assistant job. What should you do?

   A. Call (303) 555-1256.

   B. Call (828) 555-9000.

   C. Fax résumé to (414) 555-1232.

   D. Fax résumé to (828) 555-9000.

2. Which jobs require a résumé?

   A. 1 and 3

   B. 1 and 4

   C. 2 and 3

   D. 2 and 4

3. You should call if you want these jobs:

   A. 1 or 3

   B. 1 or 4

   C. 2 or 3

   D. 2 or 4

4. Which jobs require computer skills?

   A. 1 and 3

   B. 1 and 4

   C. 2 and 3

   D. 3 and 4

5. Which job requires good driving history?

   A. 1

   B. 2

   C. 3

   D. 4

150

DIRECTIONS: Look at the job application to answer the next 5 questions.
Use the Answer Sheet on page 150.

APPLICATION FOR EMPLOYMENT

Name_____ SSN_____ ①

Address_____

AVAILABILITY

Position desired _____ ②

Do you want to work: ☐ Full time? ☐ Part time?   What shift? ☐ 1st ☐ 2nd ☐ 3rd

When will you be available to begin work?_____

EDUCATION

Type of School	Name and Location	No. of Years Completed	Graduated	Degree Received (List Major)

③

EMPLOYMENT

Company name

Address

Name of supervisor

State job title and describe your work

④

6. Where do you list job experience?

   A. Part 1   C. Part 3

   B. Part 2   D. Part 4

7. Where do you put your name?

   A. Part 1   C. Part 3

   B. Part 2   D. Part 4

8. On what part do you write your availability?

   A. Part 1   C. Part 3

   B. Part 2   D. Part 4

9. On what part do you write the job you want?

   A. Part 1   C. Part 3

   B. Part 2   D. Part 4

10. Where do you write your school experience?

   A. Part 1   C. Part 3

   B. Part 2   D. Part 4

HOW DID YOU DO? Count the number of correct answers on your answer sheet. Record this number in the bar graph on the inside back cover.

Correlation Table

Student Book Pages	Workbook Pages
Pre-Unit	
2–3	
Unit 1	
4–5	2–3
6–7	4–5
8–9	6–7
10–11	8–9
12–13	
14–15	10–13
16–17	14–15
18–19	16–17
Unit 2	
20–21	18–19
22–23	20–21
24–25	22–23
26–27	24–25
28–29	
30–31	26–29
32–33	30–31
34–35	
Unit 3	
36–37	32–33
38–39	34–35
40–41	36–37
42–43	38–39
44–45	
46–47	40–43
48–49	44–45
50–51	46–47

Student Book Pages	Workbook Pages
Unit 4	
52–53	48–49
54–55	50–51
56–57	52–53
58–59	54–55
60–61	
62–63	56–59
64–65	60–61
66–67	
Unit 5	
68–69	62–63
70–71	64–65
72–73	66–67
74–75	68–69
76–77	
78–79	70–73
80–81	74–75
82–83	76–77
Unit 6	
84–85	78–79
86–87	80–81
88–89	82–83
90–91	84–85
92–93	
94–95	86–89
96–97	90–91
98–99	

Student Book Pages	Workbook Pages		Student Book Pages	Workbook Pages
Unit 7			Unit 9	
100–101	92–93		132–133	122–123
102–103	94–95		134–135	124–125
104–105	96–97		136–137	126–127
106–107	98–99		138–139	128–129
108–109			140–141	
110–111	100–103		142–143	130–133
112–113	104–105		144–145	134–135
114–115	106–107		146–147	136–137
Unit 8			Unit 10	
116–117	108–109		148–149	138–139
118–119	110–111		150–151	140–141
120–121	112–113		152–153	142–143
122–123	114–115		154–155	144–145
124–125			156–157	
126–127	116–119		158–159	146–149
128–129	120–121		160–161	150–151
130–131			162–163	